FOR MY CHILDREN

A MEMOIR

JOHN P. WALD, SR.

Outskirts Press, Inc.
Denver, Colorado

FOREWORD

By Anne-Marie Kendra and John Wald, Jr.

Our dad didn't speak of his past very often. While we knew that he had lived in a concentration camp when he was a teen, as children it was difficult for us to understand the magnitude of what that meant. The 3½ years he spent as a prisoner of the Nazis colored the way he forever looked at life. Certainly he must have suffered post-traumatic stress at many levels following the war and in the many years after. But in those days, soldiers and victims alike just picked themselves up and moved on with life.

Our family had always encouraged Dad to capture his experiences on paper, but he always resisted. It wasn't until he was in his late 60's that he finally relented. Completing his memoir was a difficult process for him; he wasn't sure he had benefited from reliving this horrific time. Still he did it for us.

During his life, he never wavered from the values in which he so strongly believed and he passed these onto us in his own way. He possessed an almost obsessive respect for the persecuted, teaching us that prejudice is wrong. He never stopped believing that any group of people, driven by fanatical leaders, could turn into barbarians, teaching us to question authority and to think for ourselves. He was fiercely patriotic, teaching us to appreciate and respect this country and our many freedoms. These messages have stayed with us.

It is in this vein that we have chosen to publish Dad's story. It is so our children and their children can learn the same lessons. It is so we, the next generation and the next, never forget.

In Memory of John P. Wald
November 16, 1927 – January 30, 2007

TO MY CHILDREN AND GRANDCHILDREN

You who have been born in America
I wish I could make you understand
What it is like not to be an American
Not to have been an American all your life
And then suddenly with the words
Of a man in flowing robes to be one.
For that moment and forever after.
One moment you belong with your fathers
To a million dead yesterdays
The next you belong with America
To a million unborn tomorrows.

George Magar Mardikian

A Favorite Story Of Dad's

Did you ever hear the story about the immigrant who came to New York and opened up a dry goods store? Well, he opened up the store and did pretty good. He got married and raised a family, a girl and a boy. His children were his pride and joy. Finally came time to retire and let the kids take over the business. OK, so he did. A few days later he walked by the store. It was closed and shuttered! Mind you, he had kept the place open for 35 years! He was shocked.

He peeked through the blinds and there were his kids running around the store with pieces of paper in their hands. He banged on the door with his fists, hollering, "Open up! OPEN UP!" His son came to the door and said, "What do you want, Pop?" "Why is the store closed?" the old man asked. "Pop, we are taking inventory." "What for are you taking inventory?" Pop cried. "We want to know what profit we've made, that's why!" said the son.

With that Pop took out $15 from his pocket and said, "Here! This is what I came with to this country. Fifteen Dollars! EVERYTHING else is profit! Now open up the store!!!"

INTRODUCTION

When I first came to this land, I was not a wealthy man!

My name is John P. Wald, formerly known as Hans Nikolas Peter Boehmerwald. I was born in Vienna, Austria, on November 16, 1927. My parents were Hans Maximilian and Anna Sophia, nee Wertheimer. They were both also born in Austria.

I came to this country with my mother on February 21, 1948. Elsie and Ernest, my mother's friends who had come to the U.S. before the war, came to pick us up from the ship, the USS Marine Tiger. I remembered them from my childhood when we all had gone hiking in the Vienna Woods, which was a long time before, in another world.

Anyway, we landed at Pier 51 on the Hudson River. We supposedly were one of the first immigrant ships put in directly at a New York City pier, instead of going to Ellis Island. With what little belongings we had, it did not take very long before we walked down the gangplank and onto U.S. soil. As long as I live I shall never forget that moment! That was the moment I became a new man in a free land!

Ernest had rented a one bedroom furnished apartment for us in the same building in which they lived on 141st Street off Broadway and Amsterdam Ave. The rent was $22 a week. No problem! We had come to this country with $30. That was all the Austrian Government would allow us to exchange Austrian currency into American dollars. So our first week's rent was covered with a little to spare for food.

I do not wish to belabor this point, but I just want you to know, that from the day we set foot in this country, no relative, no friend, nor anyone else, had to contribute to our livelihood in a financial way. The Good Lord watched over us and the prayers of well meaning people helped us over the rough spots. The kindness and moral support we received from relatives, friends and on many occasions, from complete strangers, have always been greatly appreciated. They have my most sincere thanks and gratitude. May God bless them all.

As I said, we arrived on February 21, which was a Saturday. Therefore February 22nd, George Washington's Birthday, fell on Sunday, which meant that Washington's Birthday was celebrated on Monday, February, 23rd. So it was not my fault that I couldn't go looking for a job on Monday! On Tuesday morning at last, I was on my way! First things first. I went to the Federal Court House to file my "Declaration of Intention" (also called the "First Papers") to become a Citizen of the United States. This was a long subway ride to downtown Manhattan, especially for a kid just off the boat. But, this was my first priority, to become a citizen of the United States of America, The Land of the Free and the Home of the Brave!

The afternoon before, I had decided to find Times Square, which was 100 blocks away or about five miles. Well, I walked to 42nd Street, but did not see Times Square. Then I noticed a cop directing traffic in the middle of the street and went over to him to ask him where Times Square was. "You are standing on it!" he growled and indeed I was! I looked around for a little while, glad to be there, then I walked back home. What's another five miles for a kid walking as a free man in the land of his dreams?!

What I should probably tell you is that I spoke English almost as though it were my mother tongue. When I was a child, before starting school, my parents spoke to me in English on certain days of the week, and on other days they would speak to me only in French. I did speak german[1] although it was not the main language at our house. As I grew older and went to school, german became the more common language for our family, although English and French were still used very often at home.

Walking the streets of New York looking for work was exhilarating. It was intoxicating. I was in America, a free person, amongst a free people! As luck would have it, I passed a "Help Wanted" sign in the window of a "HORN AND HARDARDT" Automat, a fast food restaurant on Broadway and 38th Street in the middle of the garment district. I went in, applied for the job and got it. The next morning I started my career as a bus boy, making $27.50 a week, plus all the food I could eat. Not bad!

This was the start of my life in America. I had dreams and would you believe it…every one came true.

---

[1] Editor's Note: The words german and germany were intentionally lower cased. Mr. Wald explains his reasoning later in his story.

MARCH 1938:
VIENNA

On March 13, 1938, Hitler's Nazis marched into Austria. german propaganda had been flooding the country for many months, telling us that the german people wanted their Austrian brothers to unite with them and become part of the german Reich. Well, that sounded pretty good to a lot of people. Indeed 98.7% of the Austrian people in a following plebiscite voted for the "Anschluss" or unification with germany. That may be most of the people, but not all. My father and many of his friends were not in favor of the germans and their ideas, and made no bones about it.

After several months, all Austrian public organizations were converted to german style or disbanded. I happened to be in the Austrian Boy Scouts. The edict went out from the Nazis to all schools: from now on the Boy Scouts will be known as "Hitler Youth." Well, my Dad was not impressed by that. In fact he told me that I was not going to join the Hitler Youth. Accordingly, I and a few other kids did not join.

The Nazis kept after us and made life pretty miserable. They repeatedly told us, "...if you don't do this, then you can't do that, etc." After a while they called us to the principal's office again and told us to tell our parents that if we did not join the Hitler Youth we could no longer go to school there. That did not sit well with my father at all! He put on his old WWI uniform with some of his medals and took me along to GESTAPO (Secret State Police) headquarters. My Dad told these people that they could not just tell his son not to go to his school any longer. Well, the GESTAPO told him that indeed they could. After some weeks they formed a school for the children of "political objectors," as they called us. The school was staffed by Jewish university professors and other politically "unreliable" individuals, who had been "dismissed" from their jobs by the Nazis. The education I received, due to the caliber of the teaching staff, was far better than that which was available at my old school. However, this whole episode earned us the attention of the Nazis. To me, my father is a hero and a great patriot, and I would not have wanted him to change his views for anybody. But what happened next was inevitable.

It started late in the evening of December 1, 1941. The SS came to our apartment building at Rembrandt Strasse 9, Wien II. Everyone had heard about the deportations to concentration camps of Jews and others who were on the Nazi's list, so my parents had a couple of suitcases packed, just in case. Well, the trucks came, and so did the Nazi-SS, with their fists banging on the door. They took us in an open truck to a grade school nearby, the one I had attended not so many years before. The Nazis had appropriated the school as a collection point for deportees. It was an odd assortment of people: Jews and Christians, including one or two other people from our parish where I had served as an altar boy for a number of years.

We stayed at this school for two days until trucks took us to the railroad station. There were several hundred people in this transport, as they called it. We were allowed to bring our suitcases. And so people and baggage were loaded tightly into boxcars. Most of us sat on our luggage. There were no toilets, just one bucket for each car. The train stopped many, many times, and waited to let other mostly troop trains pass. The prisoners - that's what the SS called us and that's what we were - were allowed out of the boxcars once a day to

2

have some thin soup made mostly from potato peels and cabbage leaves, and then loaded back on the train.

On this trip, I saw my first dead person! Some old people did not make it. They probably died from a heart attack or maybe they froze to death. They stayed right there until we were let out to eat our soup. Then the SS guards came, pulled the dead out of the boxcars and stacked them along the siding like cord wood.

DECEMBER 6, 1941 –
RIGA, LATVIA

We arrived in Latvia very early in the morning of December 6, 1941. The SS guards who had accompanied the train were lined up outside along the length of the train with their guns and dogs. With a lot of shouting and clubbing they got everyone off the train and lined up in marching order. It was a clear, cold morning. The steam from the locomotive rose straight up into the chilly air. The sky was pink and yellow and an icy blue. There was hard snow on the ground, which scrunched under our feet. All in all, it was a pretty picture in no way reflecting the misery going on all around. There were young children, babies in the arms of their mothers, grown ups and old folks. I was just past my fourteenth birthday and did not really know whether I was a grown-up or a child. However, I soon learned that being a child was very unhealthy under present conditions. I became a grown-up very quickly!

With much shouting and the use of their rifle butts the SS guards separated the women from the men. Only the really little ones were allowed to remain with their mothers. Next the guards ordered us to leave our luggage on the siding, telling us it would be brought to us shortly. Needless to say, we never saw our belongings again. And so my father and I marched off with the men, my mother with the women. Not everyone who started out made it to the camp. Stragglers, the old and the weak, were shot by the SS guards.

It turned out that we were on a railroad spur only about a mile or two from the entrance of the camp. This camp was called Jungfern Hof, a former farm containing several hundred acres of flat land, situated along the Dvina River. As I later learned, it is located about twenty miles northeast of Riga, Latvia.

When we arrived at camp, the SS assigned us to a barrack, which was already partly occupied. My father and I went inside and we found ourselves in an enormous open space. There were bunks along both long sides of the building, five high, so that the space between each bunk was only about 30 inches high. We found some empty spaces and claimed them. Down the middle of the barrack, between the bunks, were rows of long tables and benches. At the short ends of each barrack was a wood stove, which was made from an oil drum and was vented by stovepipes through the side of the building. There were a few windows high along the walls of the building, which shed enough light so that we didn't bump into each other. With all these men milling around, some of them almost in panic, it looked pretty gloomy. Good thing I was with my father to help me keep my spirits up.

After a while, the SS came and told us to get outside quickly and fall in for inspection. This was to be a ritual conducted several times a day. We were made to stand in rows, five deep. The SS men beat up a few people with their walking sticks, just to make sure that they had our full attention. Then came the "Headcount," the most important part of the inspection. So far this evening nobody had died, so the count was only of the living. In the future, if anybody died during the night, they were brought out for the first morning inspection and laid beside the column of prisoners so that they would be included in the headcount. As far as the SS was concerned a prisoner could be dead, but he must not be missing!

In the meantime, my mother along with the other women in the transport and the little children were taken to another part of the camp called the Frauen Lager or Women's Camp. It was separated from the men's camp by double rows of barbed wire about ten feet apart and eight feet high. This is where the guards walked with their dogs. There was an electrified fence all around the perimeter of the camp with guard towers every few hundred feet. The women's camp in all respects was identical to the men's. There was no special consideration given for the needs of women. Prisoners they were and that was how they were treated. I saw my mother rarely from that point on. Rarer still were the times we actually could shout a few sentences to each other from the distance. The SS guards kept us well away from the barbed wire separating our camps.

I think, at this time, I should tell you a little about my impressions of the SS. SS stands for Schutz Staffel or Protective Guard. It was formed by the early Nazis in the mid 1920's, and was intended as the core of ideological and physical shock troops of the National Socialist (Nazi) Movement. Their job was to protect the Nazi Party big wigs and their followers from left wing, so called "reactionaries," at their frequent rallies. Well, human nature being what it is, having been given a black uniform with shiny black Jack boots and some authority, these rallies often got out of hand. At any rate, the SS was much feared throughout the land.

As the war progressed and the germans occupied more and more of Eastern Europe (Poland, Slovakia, Croatia, Ukraine, etc.), certain citizens of these countries, mostly misfits, malcontents and Jew haters, volunteered to join the SS. And so it came about that we had, particularly as concentration camp guards, Latvian SS, Lithuanian SS, Ukrainian SS, etc. Yes, the german SS was very, very bad. But if you think that it would be impossible for anyone to be worse than the german SS, you would be wrong. The SS from german-occupied countries were worse!

A case in point was the Ukrainians. Before Hitler attacked Russia, the germans had made contact with the Ukrainian patriotic underground and promised them that if germany ever had it in its power, they would help them to establish an independent and free Ukraine. This had been the dream of the Ukrainian people long before the communists came to power, even back to Imperial Russia. So, this was the ultimate that anyone could promise the Ukranians. Consequently, when the Nazis invaded Russia, the Ukrainians were ready and eager to collaborate with them. To make sure that the germans appreciated their devotion to the goal to annihilate the Jews of Europe, the Ukrainian SS tried to prove themselves in every way to be as inhuman as the german SS was known to be. They succeeded!

MARCH 1942 – AUGUST 1942: LAGER JUNGFERN HOF

The Logs on the Dvina River

At about five o'clock in the morning, not yet a glimmer of dawn in the sky, we would be jolted awake by the shouts of the SS. "Everybody OUT!!! OUT!!! FALL OUT!!! LOS! LOS! RAUS! SCHNELL! SCHNELL!" This meant it was time for morning muster, to count the prisoners, dead and alive, and to line up for the day's work details. The SS men would walk along the line of prisoners, who stood five deep and count, "One, two, three, four…ten. Right face! Forward march!" The people chosen, whatever number they needed for a particular work detail, would usually, but not always, be given a slice of bread and some weak coffee to sustain them until the next meal, which was by no means certain! Most often the next meal was in the evening, and consisted of another slice of bread and some thin soup made of potato peels and cabbage leaves. The potatoes and cabbage itself, of course, was for the SS Guards. Much later I found out that it was thought that prisoners could survive on a diet of about 200 calories a day.

This early in the spring of the year, there were only two work details required. The first was the burial detail. This detail consisted of twenty men, unless there happened to be more than the usual number of dead to be buried. The normal number of dead was about five to ten per night. They died from starvation, sickness or diseases like dysentery, plus one or two who were shot by the guards just because an SS man felt so disposed. I was never on burial detail. But I heard from those who were that it was back-breaking work, consisting of digging ditches about five to six feet deep and twenty to thirty feet long. Luckily the soil was very light and sandy but it was still tough duty. Once the ditches were dug, the corpses were placed side by side in the grave and covered up with lime. After a particular grave was full, the dirt was then shoveled over them. And that was that! As a matter of fact, that is how my father was buried after he died on March 23, 1944, in the concentration camp Kaiserwald near Riga. I will tell more about my dad later.

The other work detail required a lot more people. Between one and two hundred men were sent on the "Log Kommando," as the german guards used to call it. After the "count-off" these men were marched off toward the Dvina River. I went on that work detail quite a few times. As a matter of fact, I found it very interesting to "walk" on a river. Of course, there were at least three to four feet of solid ice under my feet. The Danube in Vienna froze occasionally, and some daredevils tried to walk or even skate across it, but that was nothing like this. Later, around the middle of May, I watched the ice break up. The awesome power of nature was indescribable! So was the noise! The melt-water of snow and ice upriver caused the river to rise in its banks, which in turn caused enormous pressure to build up under the ice making it break. Great blocks of ice, some twenty, thirty feet long, crashing into each other and piling up at all different angles. After that, though only for a few moments, an SS Guard, even with a gun looked pretty puny. Such was the magic of imagination and prayer, which kept the soul alive!

Back to the logs. The guards, usually one for each ten prisoners, marched us upstream, fairly close to the shoreline. A startling feature of the landscape was a shallow ditch about a foot deep and maybe five feet across. The most striking thing about it was its color. It was blood red! This was caused by the color of the inner bark of the pine logs that were dragged down the river on the ice by hundreds of prisoners.

After we had walked a couple of hours or so, we came to the logging camp. We were allowed a brief rest before Latvian loggers came and distributed ropes with sharp hooks or clamps tied to one end. There were about five to eight people to a rope, and maybe three or four ropes to a log. And so it took about twenty prisoners to drag a log down the river! We fastened the hooks into the tree logs. And after everything was in order the SS man in charge barked an order and we lay into the ropes. To get those logs started took quit a bit of effort because they usually were frozen to the ice. We were exhausted by the time we got under way, but once in the groove it got easier.

There were at least two guards assigned to each group pulling a log. On occasion, work groups somehow got separated from each other, which could happen for many different reasons like broken ropes, etc. Prisoners would fall upon the guards, smothering their weapons with their own bodies and escape into the forest. The people who attempted such an escape were mostly locals, i.e., Latvians or Russians who could speak the language, knew the countryside and in all likelihood knew where and how to make contact with the Underground Partisans in the forests. It was a very dangerous undertaking. Many got shot in the attempt to overpower the guards. And after all that, many were recaptured by the SS and hanged. But what did we have to lose? Nothing! Nothing at all!

I never personally witnessed an escape attempt from the log kommando, but I knew when they occurred because the following morning's burial detail had to be doubled. In retribution and as a warning, the SS would hang the men in front of the assembled prisoners after the evening muster.

I have witnessed several dozen executions. Hangings were by far more brutal than executions by shooting (usually a gunshot to the back of the neck or head). Hangings were dreadful to watch and unfortunately became part of our daily lives. The gallows consisted of a long beam, about twenty feet long, supported on both sides by an "A" frame type of construction, not at all unlike a child's swing set. The long beam had six hooks on it, from which the nooses were suspended. I have seen them all occupied on several occasions.

I don't know whether it was just brutality or sheer ignorance -- our guards were amply supplied with both -- but the gallows weren't very high, so that the prisoner, when kicked off a makeshift platform, did not have very far to fall, probably not more than three or four feet. I've seen them use just a stool, which they kicked out from under the poor soul. It takes a certain distance of "drop" to achieve enough force to break a person's neck so they can mercifully die quickly. The result, therefore, was that prisoners died miserably, choking slowly to death. The SS also had the nasty habit of hanging people with the rope behind the right ear instead of the left. I've been told that by passing the rope behind the left ear, as the body's weight is applied, especially after a sufficient drop, the weight of the body either breaks the neck or the rope will pinch off the main artery to the brain, causing unconsciousness more quickly as compared to passing the rope behind the right ear. However, even this least amount of humane treatment was not accorded to us prisoners by the SS.

There was a third execution method that was also used frequently -- machine-gunning people in front of an open grave! The dreadful aspect of this kind of execution was that one might not be dead at all but only wounded with the dead falling all around and over you.

Escaping during logging was only one example of the risks prisoners took. Sometimes prisoners would smuggle a loaf of bread into the camp, obtained from one of the Latvian loggers and hidden under our clothing or amongst some kindling wood. Or someone would smuggle a pound of butter or salt pork. The mere possession of such an item was a hanging offense. Let me assure you, nobody had any illusion of what the outcome of getting caught would be. However getting the food for yourself or maybe a loved one was the overriding thought. Dying of hunger is a slow and agonizing death. We saw it happen right before our eyes every day. So if we got the opportunity, we took the risk knowing full well the consequences if caught--certain death.

To understand this willingness to take such risk, you must realize that we were totally without worth or value of any kind to the guards. To them, the more of us who died or were killed the better. Contrast that, if you will, with the value of a slave in America in pre-Civil War times. Pardon me for using the "S" word but I do not know of any nation or culture on the face of this earth, which did not practice slavery at one time or another in its history. But always, throughout history, a slave had value of some kind to his master. We had no value of any kind. And so, if we did things far out of proportion, gain vs. risk, you'll understand why. Normal values did not apply. And so spring slowly wore into summer. Despite our surroundings, we tried to survive from one day to the next, even though the cost may have been high.

Days, weeks and months slowly rolled by without any change in our condition whatsoever. We had very little news of the outside world. On occasion the SS acted particularly brutal with shooting sprees or hanging a few more people than they ordinarily would. We hoped that their ill humor was caused by some bad news from the front. However, early 1942 was still the time of steady german advances, with very few setbacks. Stalingrad and other decisive defeats of the germans by the Russian Army and Allies were still way in the future.

In early spring I had been assigned to an old, Hungarian carpenter, Mr. Horvath, as an apprentice. I did not realize it at the time, but this fortunate happenstance had a great deal to do with my ultimate survival. Besides a few songs and Hungarian phrases, I learned a great deal from that kindly old man. I learned to respect and love tools. I learned how to make a square cut on a piece of wood. And I learned how to recognize and to respect a craftsman. A craftsman, whether they are a carpenter, physician or salesman, in the larger sense of the word, is anyone who really knows what he or she is doing. He also taught me that there was no such thing as a "good tool." I'd ask Mr. Horvath to please give me a good saw or hammer or whatever I needed, and he would tell me, "There is no such thing as a 'good saw,' you must work it right and if you do, it will be a good saw!"

One day, as I was carrying a few pieces of lumber on my shoulder, past the Kommandant's Headquarters, I saw this boy, maybe ten or twelve years old, watering the trees and bushes around the front of the building. All of a sudden this big burly SS man came down the stairs, grabbed the kid and started to beat and kick him mercilessly. Frightened and weak as he was, the boy did not struggle very long. It was over very quickly. I couldn't help but think what that SS man should deserve for that brutal deed.

After a few months of being a carpenter's helper, I was assigned to work with the camp electrician. This was of great and lasting benefit to me as well. First of all it gave me the opportunity to again work at a trade. It also got me away from digging ditches or loading or unloading railroad cars or coal barges. I learned how to string wires for lights in the barracks and other areas throughout the camp. I also had to learn to strap on climbing irons and climb up to the top of the power poles, which were positioned all along the perimeter of the camp. They were equipped with floodlights to light up the barbed wire fences. I can tell you, it can be pretty scary to go up a light pole during a thunderstorm or in the dark to change a light bulb. In addition, we always had to be mindful of some trigger-happy guard, either on the ground or in one of the watch towers along the fence.

The Theorem of Pythagoras

Often, between work details in the morning or late afternoon, the guards had us fall out on the grounds between our barracks for no particular reason. Sometimes they'd search the barracks for whatever

13

they imagined they would find as contraband. These searches would go on for hours on end. Or they'd just have us stand there doing nothing for hours. Among us we had a lot of teachers, university professors, and other academics who had gotten kicked out of their teaching positions by the Nazis and deported because they were Jews or otherwise did not fit in with the german regime. These teachers took a few of us youngsters, there probably were no more than five or six of us in the entire camp, under their wing to teach us what circumstances deprived us from learning. Our classroom was an open field with armed guards walking up and down. The teachers would talk to us about whatever subject they had in mind. Obviously, there was no "lesson plan" or any kind of formal structure. There were no books, paper or pencils. If a particular subject required a graphic depiction or visualization, we did it as best we could in the sand. And if a guard came too near we had to erase it or make believe we were just staring at the sand.

Believe me, these few minutes at a time of learning were precious and still to this day I owe much of what I was able to achieve in life to these courageous teachers who risked being shot instantly by the guards had they been caught in their endeavor. The teachers probably did it to maintain their own sanity as much as to educate us. And so I learned algebra and geometry in the sand.

Other subjects were taught on the way to and from work, such as history and geography. You would try to line up in your marching order next to a teacher, if possible. Don't imagine that all this happened on a regular or scheduled basis. It all happened whenever and however possible. And despite the constant hunger and ever-present danger, it was done in great earnest on the part of the teacher on the one hand, and with great desire to learn by the student on the other. It was after all an opportunity to transport oneself consciously or subconsciously away from the here and now, even if only briefly, into a realm of normalcy! It felt good, at least to me it felt good. I do not believe that I've been taught nor have I learned with as much dedication since. May the Good Lord reward these teachers for their unselfish dedication.

AUGUST 1942 TO JULY 1943:
RIGA GHETTO

In mid August, 1942, the rumors started that the prison camp at Jungfern Hof was going to be closed down. Exactly when, nobody knew for certain. Sure enough, at the end of August word came down, "Tomorrow we move!"

The next morning a long line of open trucks arrived just as we were standing in front of our barracks for the morning headcount. We were told to go and get our belongings such as they were, and come right back out again. After a while the SS officer in charge of the camp made a short speech telling us not to worry, that we were being transferred to another camp not far away. We did not know if we should believe the man or not. We knew that there were occasions when prisoners were told they were being moved, got on trucks and were never seen again. We would find out much later that they had all been machine-gunned. So we did not know whether the SS officer was only telling us this story in order to prevent a panic amongst us two thousand or so prisoners.

We boarded the trucks with considerable trepidation. After about a half hour, we came to the outskirts of a city. Some of the prisoners recognized the place and said we were riding through the outskirts of

Riga. One can imagine our relief, as we allowed ourselves to think that we might live a little while longer. We continued on into the city. In those days we still wore our civilian clothes. (The striped prison garb came later.) In this way our passage through the city did not cause too much of a stir. Finally the trucks drove through a barbed wire gate, which had been put up right across a big street. On either side, the barbed wire fences stretched as far as we could see, guarded by SS with guns ordered to shoot anyone who came near the fences.

We had arrived at the Jewish ghetto in Riga. It was an old neighborhood in which Jews had lived for many hundreds of years. It was common in Europe during the Middle Ages, and especially in Eastern Europe, for Jews to congregate or assemble in a particular part of town. This occurred more often than not by decree of the Czar or other local ruler. But also because their gentile neighbors did not welcome them with open arms, so they were forced by circumstances to seek their own kind to live with. It can be argued that being made to live in close proximity with each other allowed the Jews to adhere to and thus preserve their laws and traditions, more so than if they had been dispersed. I hope that this theory is not going to be put to the test because thanks to Hitler's "Final Solution" there are now not enough Jews left in Europe to populate a ghetto!

By putting one or even two families to a room there was enough space for all the people from the Jungfern Hof work camp. This of course meant that our family was reunited! Even under these sad circumstances it was wonderful to be together again! With luck, we were assigned a tiny little room to ourselves. There was no furniture, just mattresses on the floor. My father scrounged a large box, which we used as a table.

Some of the former inhabitants were still around to tell us about german brutality; shootings and hangings and deportation to slave labor camps in germany. As far as food was concerned, we were on very slim rations. We received some bread and corn meal, also some beans and occasionally potatoes and cabbage. Butter, eggs, meat or sugar were unheard of! My mother managed with what they provided to cook at least one meal a day, which we ate together in the evening. The cooking was done on a coal stove in the kitchen of the apartment shared by, if my recollection serves, 15 to 20 persons. The one bathroom was shared by three other apartments on the floor. Remember also, one apartment equaled three families.

Work details, or "kommandos" as we called them, were pretty much chance and luck. The prisoners were lined up in rows of five. And if a particular job, say to unload three box cars, required fifty people, the Capo (Camp Police), would count off ten rows of five people and off they went. My poor mom and dad usually got miserable work details. There was nothing but hard work with not a mouthful of food to scrounge or beg. Most of the work consisted of hard labor with brutal guards constantly on your back. And the rules were as always: The headcount must be correct! It did not matter whether the bodies were dead or alive. And so it went.

The following story depicts events I did not witness myself. However, they were told to me by persons, who to the best of my knowledge, were eyewitnesses to the events described. I did, however, see the outcome of these events with my own eyes.

A few weeks before our arrival from Jungfern Hof, but shortly after the establishment of the Riga Ghetto, the Nazi SS lined up all the Jews in the streets. The SS waded through these terrified people, shooting them at random. I heard that the SS grabbed little babies from their mother's arms, swung them by their legs and smashed their heads against the walls of buildings. I was told that blood ran in the gutters and dripped from the walls. For a fact I saw the blood stains on the curbs and on the walls of houses, visual evidence attesting to the truth of the stories I had heard. Can you imagine the sound of guns, the cries of the people and the desperation of the poor mothers as their children were ripped away from them by these Nazi monsters? The trouble is I can. Only too well!

My Latvian Friend Jan

On rare occasions there were special work details based on certain skills. Lucky for me, I was picked to work as an electrician, a trade I had learned in Jungfern Hof. Off I went one morning, along with about twenty-five other men who were carpenters, to work at a furniture factory. There I was assigned as a helper to a kindly fellow named Jan, a Latvian civilian, about thirty years old. He taught me a lot about the trade. I learned a lot from him as a human being as well. But best of all he brought me some bread and cheese or a little piece of sausage most every day! So during the few months that I worked with Jan, I was hardly ever really, really hungry. I ate what Jan gave me and gave my camp rations to my parents. That was the way my parents wanted it, because they did not want me to smuggle anything into camp. The chances of getting caught by the SS and consequently hung were just too great as they searched us each night upon our return to camp.

Almost as wonderful as the food was the relative freedom I enjoyed for those few months while working with Jan. We were not tied to a single work place, such as a workbench or shop. We were able to move freely throughout the factory buildings as our work required. On rare occasions, if we had to work at an outlying warehouse, which was maybe three or four miles away, Jan got bicycles for us to ride back and forth. Jan knew it would make me happy to once again ride a bicycle like a real person! I was glad that my Dad had taught me how to ride. This now seemed so many years ago that my dad had taken me to the Prater, an amusement park in Vienna's 2nd District. There one could rent a bike and that is where I learned to ride.

One time Jan took me home to his apartment. I had not been inside a real home in so long, and it was such a strange feeling. It was hard to relax because I was concerned about Jan and his family. There would be real trouble if someone saw me and reported it to the authorities. But Jan was not afraid. Jan introduced me to his wife, whom I said I thought was his daughter. I was so embarrassed by my mistake, but my mother, when I told her about it, assured me that the lady was surely not insulted. My mother was right, because after that, I'd occasionally find a hard-boiled egg in my lunch bag, which Jan brought from home!

I'm telling you about Jan and his family -- God bless them -- to remind myself that even in those terrible times there were people who acted like Human Beings! So, during that time of five or six months even though I had to go back to the barbed wire and the guards every night, for a few hours every day Jan made it possible for me to feel like a Person instead of a prisoner!

JULY 1943 TO AUGUST 1943:
KZ KAISERWALD BY RIGA

O ne day in July 1943 all outside kommandos stopped! That meant nobody left the ghetto to go to work outside. We were completely cut off from the outside world. The guards were increased, which was really frightening. Then rumors of all kinds started to make the rounds, none of them good. Hitler's armies were on a rampage, both in the east and in the west. From what we knew, an early end to the war was entirely unlikely.

Finally, word came down that the germans were shutting down the ghetto and we were to be transferred to another camp. Where that might be nobody knew. Considering that the SS might have killed us right where we were, going to another camp was the lesser of evils.

One day the trucks came. Many trucks. They had come to haul us off to some unknown place. The fact, that there were trucks meant that the trip was probably rather short. There was a railroad spur right into the ghetto, which one might suppose would be used for a longer trip. The fact that the trucks were not open lorries but enclosed trucks did not assuage our fears. We knew of cases where guards connected the exhaust pipe of the truck into an inlet of the enclosed compartment and suffocated the prisoners. And that was the end of their journey.

As it turned out, my parents and I boarded a truck and less than an hour later arrived at KZ Kaiserwald alive! This camp was located on the eastern outskirts of Riga. As soon as we arrived, my mother was separated from us once again.

They took us men to a large building all open on the inside. There we had to strip down to the skin, leaving our clothes in a pile. This obviously was an anxious time for any one who still had any kind of valuables with him. What to do? You can't take it with you because where can you hide anything? At any rate, this was not my father's problem nor mine. We had nothing to sweat over.

We were all issued striped prison uniforms. They came in two sizes, large and small. Whatever did not fit, one cut off or rolled up. Most were way too large. Along with the prison garb we were given a number! I do not remember exactly, but it was a five or six digit number preceded by a red triangle. The red triangle stood for enemies of the state. After the war, we were referred to as political prisoners.

New things kept breaking all around us. In order to make the new Kaiserwald Concentration Camp run more efficiently, the germans had imported Criminals with a capital "C" from some prison nearby to be our barracks chiefs. They were convicted thieves and murderers -- mostly murderers. Now these criminals had a number on their chest also, preceded by a yellow triangle. Other categories were purple for Jehovah's Witnesses, Seventh Day Adventists and Quakers. Blue was for Gypsies and other folk.

At this time, very few work details went outside the camp, consequently very little food was to be scrounged anywhere, not even a few rotten potatoes or cabbage leaves from a garbage can. So, we were very hungry all the time.

To amuse themselves the guards invented a game: Pigeons! They had a box or crate about three feet on a side and about two feet high. They gave us a handful of corn and told us boys to prop up the box with a stick, which was tied to a string. They told us to put a few kernels of corn under the box. When a pigeon went under the box to get the corn, we were told to yank the string. If the bird was caught, we had to reach under the box, catch the bird and hand it to the guard. The guard then went to the guard shed or our barracks, whichever was closer, and with the bird in his hand used the door to decapitate the poor animal and allow its blood to run over his hands.

This may give you an idea as to what kind of people our guards really were. But like my grandfather said: "Human beings are all right, but people stink!" I found this to be true many times over throughout my life.

AUGUST 1943 TO FEBRUARY 1944:
WORK CAMP SCHLOCK BY RIGA

One morning without warning, as we were standing at "parade" for headcount the SS counted off a few hundred people, me included, and told us to get ready to move out. We went and got our blankets and mess kits, and again lined up outside the barracks. After a while, there came the trucks. We were loaded up and off we went. We did not know where we were going. We could not help but fear for our lives. And so, we just sat in the bed of the trucks and prayed and hoped for the best. We were on our way to Schlock, about 70-80 miles from Riga.

I did not know at the time that my mother also had been selected for that move. My father was not and stayed behind in Kaiserwald. This was probably because we were not in the same barracks and therefore we did not line up together.

Schlock was a dreary place in northwest Latvia, not far from the Baltic Sea. There was a pulp mill out in the middle of nowhere. A railroad spur and a dirt road was all that connected it to the rest of the world. There was a barbed wire fence and a few watch towers. But in reality, they were not needed to keep us from escaping. We were in the middle of a vast pine forest and a coastal swamp to the north. Where could we go? We would not have had the strength anyway. And even if we did, what then?

I saw my mother on rare occasions, and then only while she was at work. One of the times I saw her she was unloading railroad boxcars. She was in a line of women prisoners unloading bags of stuff, probably 40-50 lb bags of sulfur or lime used in the manufacture of paper. Only God knows how that frail woman, who never weighed more than 110 lbs at her best, managed to do that day after day.

As for me, most of what I did was moving pine logs. The logs got moved either by pulling sleds when the ground was hard enough or by dragging them along ruts, which had been carved by many years usage. All this, of course, as all our labors, was done under the constant shouting and whip of our SS guards.

Winter is long and hard in northern Latvia, especially if you don't have enough food to put in your belly. It lasts from October to the end of May. None of us thought we were going to survive to see the spring, which was an unimaginably long time away. For that matter, so was tomorrow morning!

The Russian POWs

We had seen Russian Prisoners of War on several previous occasions marching along to work or in the back of trucks. At Schlock, however, the germans had put a Russian POW camp right next to ours. The Russians were treated as bad or even worse (if that was possible) than we were. They were made to work like animals. They were beaten by their german guards and starved to death. Naturally we took every opportunity to make contact with them and talk with them. In those days I spoke Russian quite fluently and so we tried to cheer each other up. I remember the Russian soldiers saying to us: "Nietechwo nie bajusa. Fsijo buidit f'damoy," which meant, "Nothing to be afraid of. Soon we'll be home." We hoped that they were right, although it is likely that they knew less about what was going on in the outside world than we did.

In the evening the Russians POWs would sing old Russian folk songs. I had heard the songs in the camps before and knew them well. You have not heard "The Volga Boatmen" sung like I've heard it sung by a bunch of Cossacks in the still of the evening from far away. You look at the barbed wire and you begin to look through it and after a while the barbed wire is not there at all! Pretty soon we joined in from our side of the fence. "Volga, Volga, Matj Radnajah" meaning, "Volga, Volga Mother of Our Land." Then we sang, "Shirakah Stranah Moja Radnaja," the Russian equivalent of "This Land is Your Land, This Land is My Land!" We also sang some Russian Army songs like, "Jesly saftra voynah, Jesly saftra pychot! Na semlje, na besah, e na more," meaning "If tomorrow there is war, tomorrow we'll be on our way! On the land, in the sky and on the sea!" The germans, of course, would have coughed up a brick had they known what we were singing about!

These rare "sing-alongs" really gave such a lift to our spirits that is hard to imagine. While I am sad to say I've a very poor ear for music, these plaintive melodies in some songs and very stirring in others meant an awful lot to me. I remember them well to this day. My poor wife, children, grandchildren and in-laws have been subjected to my rendition of all of these songs!

While I am on the subject of music and spiritual things, I have to tell you about other times going back to Jungfern Hof, when music, though sad and solemn, was part of my life. On Friday evenings after we ate and everybody was settled down, a group of ten Jewish men would gather. At times it was difficult to find ten men who could still stand up! The most important part of the service was the Kaddish, the Prayer for the Dead. I've heard it many, many times, "Vejiskadal, vejiskadat shemeh rabboh."

Besides Russian and a little Polish, I also spoke Yiddish quite well. And of course English, whenever possible! In the camps most everybody endeavored to speak anything but german, the language of murderers! I must say, that the german language did have a considerable influence though, in my progress as a child. My mother, being a literature buff, recited Schiller's poems and Goethe's Faust to me instead of nursery rhymes. I can still do a goodly portion of Faust's "Prologue in Heaven" from memory. Along those lines, it is still a mystery to me how a people so advanced in many respects could sink so low under the influence of a relatively few fanatical leaders. In my mind, the higher one regards the cultural achievements of a people, the Schillers and Goethes, etc. of a nation, the more one must abhor the depth to which that nation has sunk! Consequently I've never thought it worthwhile to teach my children to speak german. Maybe that was a mistake, but be that as it may!

FEBRUARY TO AUGUST 1944: KZ KAISERWALD BY RIGA

As I said before, my mother and I had been sent to the Work Camp Schlock. My father remained in KZ Kaiserwald. In mid-February 1944, our camp was closed down and all the living prisoners were trucked back to Kaiserwald. I went looking for my father and inquired about him from people I thought might know anything about him. Remember, this was a vast camp with dozens of barracks or "blocks" with hundreds of prisoners in each.

I happened on him a few days after my return. When I saw him, he was in terrible shape. He was barely able to walk, even to get his daily ration of potato-peel soup and one slice of bread. One prisoner could not obtain someone else's ration. Get it yourself or die! I was not assigned to the same barracks as my father so I was not with him during his time of agony.

When I was able to go to his barracks to see him after work in the evening, he did not recognize me. He lay on the lower bunk of a three-bunk tier and just kept clawing the air and mumbling words, which I could not understand. I tried to comfort him, but there was nothing I could do or say other than try to hold his hand and pray that the good Lord would soon grant him rest and peace. I knew that this was the end for my dad. I knew, because I had seen so many people die. You can see Death in a person's face, but mostly in their eyes. I had to leave my dad after only a short while at about five thirty or so, this being the end of March, because anybody caught outside the barracks after dark was shot on sight. Staying over night was impossible also, because turning up missing at the nightly bed check was a hanging offense.

MARCH 23, 1944:THE DAY MY DAD DIED

The next evening, when I came to my dad's barracks his bunk was empty! He was gone! He had been buried in one of the mass graves I described earlier – open pits dug by prisoners, covered with lime and closed when full. I never knew where my father's grave was located as these graves weren't marked.

My children ask me, "Dad, how did you feel?" "What did you think?" What I felt was that my dad was lucky to be out of this infernal misery! And what I thought was that by tomorrow I'd probably be dead also. And if not tomorrow, surely the day after! Given the circumstances I did not mourn the death of my father. Instead I would not have minded at all to be in his place! This experience and frustration at our utter helplessness did increase my hatred and contempt for the Nazis and everyone who wore a german uniform or was in any way connected with the Nazis. Not so my parents. I believe that they, with their last conscious thought, prayed for their enemies. I hoped that they prayed for me also. I was then sixteen years old.

Now that I am a father myself, I think back and try to imagine how my father and my mother must have felt seeing their only child in a concentration camp with all that implied. My father was a very brave man, no doubt about that. I am certain that he did not regret anything he did to preserve and defend what he considered the right and dignity of human beings. But, I'm sure that in his heart of hearts, he must have wondered what on earth he could have done or should have done that he did not do, that might have prevented the tragedy, which befell his family. I'm sure the Good Lord has granted him the peace, which he so well deserved.

It just so happened that I was able to talk to my mother on that day. I spotted her walking along the barbed wire double fence, which ran between the men's and women's camps. I had to shout to her the sad news that my father had died. She took it much the same way as I did earlier. There really was little we could say, except hope that this Nazi hell would end one day soon.

During the coming months I very seldom saw my mother. It was even rarer that we were actually able to speak to each other. Without watches it was very difficult to keep to any sort of schedule. Moreover, the guards kept us moving along the fence continuously, and would not allow us to stand in one spot for any length of time. It was very difficult to argue with a bayonet, especially if you knew that it would be used without any hesitation, as I had seen done on too many occasions. To get jabbed with a bayonet was almost certain death. Even if the wound was relatively slight, the loss of blood would weaken a person to the point where one would be unable to work or even get one's ration! Not to speak of the almost certainty of infection under the conditions in which we lived. It was a slow death, unless the guard felt inclined to put the person he had stabbed with his bayonet out of his misery with a bullet in the head. In either event, the guard would have been considered to have done his duty and if anything would have been in line for a commendation!

While I am chronicling daily events, I will tell you about the time I was assigned to a work detail near the Guards' barracks. I saw a guard grab a boy about fifteen years old, a walking skeleton, (there were no little kids left by this time). He put him between his knees, put a garden hose into his mouth and drowned him. This was not a noisy death, but it was a violent one, with the poor boy thrashing around and finally letting go of his life between the legs of this brute. It came to me at that time that the difference between animals and people is that animals kill, for the most part, only because they are hungry or to defend themselves. They have to eat to survive or protect their own. On the other hand, people kill because they are vicious! To kill their enemies may be justifiable by the laws of nature, but to torture their victims is most certainly not. Just remember what my grandfather taught me: "Human beings are all right, but people stink!!" That is why, Lord knows, I love ANIMALS! Especially dogs!

We knew little (at least I knew little) about the siege of Leningrad or the defeat of the germans at Stalingrad. I did not know about D-Day at Normandy on June 6th, 1944. I did not know about the failed attempt on Hitler's life on July 20th, 1944. News was scarce, especially after the outside work kommandos stopped, which meant that the last contact with the outside world was gone. Yet we kept on hoping that the end to the war would be swift.

AUGUST 1944 TO SEPTEMBER 1944 - KZ STUTTHOF BY DANZIG

Again it was time for us to move. By now our numbers had dwindled to probably no more than 1000-1500 people left alive at Concentration Camp Kaiserwald. The germans were really getting antsy because by now the Russian Red Army had taken back most of the territory the germans had conquered. The Americans, British and French were ready to launch their offensive thrust into germany! The Allied Air Forces were bombing the german cities to smithereens! Berlin, Hamburg, Bremen, Dresden, etc. It sounded great! It could not be any better!! However, all that really made our precarious hold on life even more tenuous, because as the war was brought to their home front, the germans had fewer and fewer resources, and less and less incentive to keep us alive.

So this was the situation at the time the germans evacuated our Camp at Kaiserwald. The guards lined us up at the railroad siding inside the camp. After several hours a line of boxcars backed onto the siding and we were loaded up. The scene was the usual -- the SS guards shouting, cursing and kicking and using their rifle butts to get everyone onto the train. There was also the usual number of dead along the siding, but that was to be expected.

I don't remember how many days we spent on the train from Riga, Latvia, to Danzig, in eastern germany, a distance of about 250 miles. It probably was three or four days. There was hardly any food or water. There was a bucket per railroad car for sanitation. There were about 80-100 people in each box car. We stopped once or twice a day to get out and receive our ration of soup or black coffee. We stopped more often to pull over at a siding to let another train pass. Troop trains going to the front, trains with wounded going to the rear. The guards used to make us sit down in the box cars when a train passed so that we could not look out the windows, which were way up high on the wall of the cars. But usually someone took a chance to sneak a look, cost what may. We just had to know what was going on. Finally, we arrived at Konzentrations Lager Stutthof by Danzig.

So far I had only been in concentration camps were people died of hunger and disease, or from being shot or hung for any so called offense whatsoever. This was different. This was an *extermination* camp. The gas chambers and crematoriums were going day and night. I am sure one could see the eerie glow above the crematorium chimneys from miles and miles away. There were, of course, towns and villages all around KZ Stutthof, as there were around most other concentration camps, such as Buchenwald and Dachau. There were over one hundred camps within germany and the german occupied territories. The fires of the crematoriums as well as the smell of burning flesh were unmistakable. And yet after the war one could not find a german or Pole or Ukrainian or any of my brave Austrian compatriots who had ever heard of such a thing, let alone who had been a member of the Nazi party!!

This was a really stark place. Barbed wire and watch towers in every direction. Row after row of wooden barracks. Not a tree in sight, not even grass! If ever there was any grass, it had long ago been trampled into the dirt by thousands upon thousands of feet. And towering above, were all the chimneys of the crematorium. I did not know where my mother was or even whether she was still alive. Had she come to Stutthof or was she brought to another camp? Did she make it out of Kaiserwald?

My fellow prisoners were walking skeletons moving about, marching in columns as the guards commanded. Others were in groups moving piles of rocks from one place to another. There were no more outside work details; nobody left the camp. Through it all, we saw the constant movement of trains of boxcars, coming into the camp and leaving empty. We knew of course what that meant, although nobody spoke about it. Train loads of people were brought in to be gassed and burned. We expected our turn to come any day. Probably tomorrow!

My Guardian Angel

Things were pretty chaotic in the camp. No work, very, very little food. Although the Red Army, as the Russian Forces were properly referred to, had crossed the Polish frontier there was little relief for us. They were still hundreds of miles away. Our guards, the germans, and their mercenaries were as ruthless as ever. Let us not make any mistake about it -- they were carrying out the directives of their leaders and they in turn were carrying out the will of the german people!

And so on this day in mid August 1944 I was marching along in a column of prisoners as I had done many times before. We were marching up one camp street and down another, for what seemed a long time. Then we stopped. It sank in only very slowly exactly where we were. We had halted in front of the entrance to the "Brause Bad," as a sign said. That was german for the "Showers!" But we knew that the place was not used for showers -- this was the Gas Chamber. Incredibly, as I recall, nobody panicked. I believe we were all so weak from hunger and exhaustion we were beyond caring. The guards just herded us into the place and we just went inside. From my recollection the chamber was about fifty feet long and about thirty wide. It had a low ceiling with shower heads along the length of it. The single door through which we came had a small spur railroad track leading into the building. On the track, almost near the rear wall of the building stood a cart. This cart looked like a baggage cart, as I'm sure you have seen at railroad stations. There was only one cart there. The rest probably were outside. These carts were used to move the corpses out of the gas chamber to the ovens.

I noticed that cart the moment I walked into the chamber and a strong voice in my mind told me, "Go back there, get hold of that cart and push it out the door! Now! Quick!" I did just that. I pushed the cart through the doors and the doors closed behind me. I pushed the cart, as though that was my job, onto a little siding and left it there. I mixed in with the other prisoners, milling around there and was gone! I thank the Good Lord who sent my Guardian Angel to rescue me at that hour. And so it was that I did not die that day!

SEPTEMBER 1944 TO MARCH 1945: WORK CAMP ROSTOW, GERMANY

In early September the germans moved us again, several hundred of us, this time to Rostow, a small railroad town about two hundred miles due west of Danzig. The town was situated about 15 miles from the Baltic Sea. At the time, of course I had no idea exactly where it was, except that we were now in northern germany, not too far from Denmark. Our camp was a barbed wire enclosure, near the railroad yards. It consisted of some old warehouse like structures with some bomb damage here and there.

In the middle of December, American armies fought the Battle of the Bulge (12/16/44), Hitler's last attempt at a massive counter attack on the western front. It failed, thank God! In the camps, we did not know about this battle or for that matter about any others. I merely mention it here, as I did others before, to put our situation in some form of historical context.

The germans put most of us to work on various projects in the railroad yard. I was assigned work on an electric power line through the middle of town, which had been destroyed by Allied bombing. Lacking any sort of power equipment, like augers or trenchers, we were made to dig the trenches for the poles with picks and shovels.

The trenches were about two feet wide, eight feet long and about six to eight feet deep. Then came the time to put up the pole. I was in that detail, since I was the "electrician." None of us had ever put up power poles, so we had to figure it out as we went along. We were about twenty-five to thirty men, such as we were. Scarecrows all! We maneuvered the thick end of the pole over the ditch the long way, so that the fat end was protruding out over the length of the ditch. Then we took a piece of board and stuck it down into the ditch at the far end of the pole, so that the heel of the pole would be up against the board. When we lifted the pole, first by pulling up on it, then with ropes, the pole would slide down the board and we were able to get it to an upright position. Each pole took us several days. With several dozen poles to put up it took several months to just to get the poles up. To the best of my knowledge the line was never finished, at least not by us.

On rare occasions some germans, mostly old women, because that was all that was left of them by that time, would smile at us and try to say some encouraging words. Rarer still one would put a crust of bread or something to eat by the side of the road. They would have to put it close enough for us to reach without going too far from our work area. Stepping out of line was risking to get shot. In all fairness, I must say these kind people, may God bless them, also put themselves at risk. If a guard caught them giving us anything to eat, or even talking to us they would scream at them or use their rifle butts to push these civilians away.

Many days and nights we saw Russian bombers fly over the city. Occasionally, they dropped bombs. There were many fires that we could see from the camp as well as some of the damage caused by the bombs in town. Somehow our camp, although it was right next to the railroad yard, was never bombed! And so with the grace of God some of us survived!

MARCH TO APRIL 1945:
KZ STUTTHOF BY DANZIG

W ith the war coming closer and closer every day it was obvious to us that our days in Rostow were numbered. Although the front was coming closer it was still many hundreds of miles away. Therefore, we knew that there was no chance that the Russians would overrun the germans and liberate us before the germans had a chance to move us again. And move us they did again, using the usual boxcars, with which we had become so familiar over the years. Much to our surprise and alarm the train moved east. This did not bode well at all. Why would the germans move us east, since they did not want us to fall into Russian hands, unless they wanted to kill us!

We traveled for several days under the usual hardships, which I have described before. Except that food was even scarcer, if that is possible, and the guards more short tempered. At the end of this journey, much to our surprise, we wound up at the KZ Stutthof by Danzig. german concentration camps, no matter how forbidding, showed signs of discipline, which one would expect in a prison. Stutthof at that time was a mess! Although the watch towers were manned and the fences electrified, there were few SS to be seen inside the camp. The dead and dying were lying in the streets along the barracks. Food distribution was sporadic and on many days there was none. There was only one headcount in the morning instead the usual two or three. One day we found a horse in the compound. That poor horse probably was more dead than alive when it somehow wandered in. We ate that horse down to the bones and then we charred the bones over a fire and gnawed on those till there was nothing left. I'm sure that horse helped a number of us, including me, survive for a few more days.

The quest to survive is a basic instinct or attribute of all living creatures. Be it a weed by the side of the road or an antelope being hunted by a lion or a human being subjected to intolerable circumstances. Somehow that flame, that will to survive, lives on. We hung on from day to day and from week to week for almost two months until the germans decided to move us again.

APRIL 28 1945:
THE ISLAND OF RUEGEN
IN THE BALTIC SEA

We came here from the Concentration Camp Stutthof near Danzig, germany, about 200 miles to the east. It is now called Gdansk and has belonged to Poland since the end of World War II. We came here in three coal barges, which were pulled by a single tug boat, the holds filled with prisoners. There was just enough space to sit or stand, but not to lie down. We had started out with what I'd guess to be about 3000 souls from Stutthof. By the time we reached Ruegen there were maybe 2000 to 2500 of us left alive. The SS marched us from the dock for several miles; the weak just dropping by the wayside. If they were dead, they were just left there and nobody noticed. But if they were still alive the nearest SS guard walked over and kicked the prisoner to make him get up. If that encouragement did not produce the desired result, the german would shoot that person in the back of the head. As we marched along we avoided direct eye contact with the SS men as much as possible in order not to draw attention to ourselves, which inevitably would spell disaster.

We walked some number of miles like in a dream (I did not know the word zombies then). One foot in front of the other, one foot in front of the other, on and on, as long as these bones would hang together, until we finally came to this place. There were no barracks or huts or anything. All I could see was barbed wire all around, a holding pen of some sort. We laid down on the ground exhausted. After a while they pulled in a field kitchen and began to dish out some thin soup and a slice of bread for the prisoners. This was our first food in about eight days. That is for those of us who still had the strength to stand in line to get it! I was one of them! Thank God! It is amazing how even a few scraps of food could mean the difference between life and death, literally! And so it went for the next couple of days, sleeping out in the open, freezing. After all, it was early spring in the Baltics.

APRIL 30, 1945:
RUEGEN CAMP

O ne day, they loaded whatever number of us was left after the march into a coal barge. Now they needed only one barge! We had started out with about 3000 souls from Stutthof. And now as they pushed us into the holds like sardines, I think there were probably fewer than a thousand of us left. There was no place to sit or lay down. The strongest, of course, got the lion's share of the available space. In addition to us concentration camp prisoners, the SS also loaded a few dozen Norwegian prisoners of war aboard the barge. The barge was pulled by an ocean-going tug boat, which also had the SS guards on board. During the night of April 30th, the Norwegian prisoners of war cut the barge loose from the tug. We were floating free! Our location was about 40 miles southeast of Denmark and maybe 60 miles south of Sweden. At that time the British forces had already liberated that area of Denmark and of course, Sweden was free. So it was our goal, to reach shore at either place!

But what course? To our good fortune we had the Norwegian prisoners on board. As soon as they cut loose of the tug, they asked for volunteers to stand on top of the barge's flat deck and hold up blankets to catch the wind by which they would steer the barge.

Unfortunately the winds and the tides were not in our favor. We drifted for about a hundred miles almost due west. At some point of our journey we were probably no more than a few miles off the Danish coast. Then, however, the wind and currents changed and we drifted south. We ran aground, I'd say about 100 - 150 yards off shore, about five miles north of the german town of Neustadt-in-Holstein. Again we had spent several days without food or water. While at sea, some of the people had tied belts or strings together and dropped pots or other containers over the side to get some sea water to drink. I believe I tried it but I did not have much of it as someone earnestly warned us against drinking seawater. And, I didn't have too much of it because the ones who wanted to drink it were bigger than me! In the end, I probably was better off for not having much of it.

MAY 2, 1945:
MORNING ON A BEACH IN
SCHLESWIG-HOLSTEIN
AND MARCH TO NEUSTADT

The barge ran aground about 100 yards off shore. I don't know what happened to the Norwegian prisoners of war. To the best of my knowledge they were not there at that time. Being in a lot better physical shape than we were, they probably just took off when they had the chance. And I certainly can't fault them for that! Not having eaten anything in many days drove a number of our people to go ashore in search of food. You have to remember that the war was still on and that meant this was enemy territory. At this time of the year there were no crops of potatoes or beets or anything to eat from the fields, so they probably stole some chickens and other food stuff from barns, I suppose. I was not there. I did not have the strength to go. The locals raised the alarm with local police, and I can't say I blame them. It must have been a sight to see a few dozen virtual skeletons chasing a few chickens!

On board the barge, there was finally enough space to stretch out and get some sleep, since many had gone ashore. I dimly perceived in my own subconscious mind that this was not the end of our troubles. I just knew there was more to come. Sure enough, shortly after daybreak we heard shooting. When I say "we" I mean Joe Weinberg and I. Joe and I had been together for almost a year. From one camp to another, sharing whatever little we had. The SS was on shore shooting and yelling for everyone to come ashore. People started to climb up on the deck of the barge and just hunker down and look as inconspicuous as possible. That of course did not work. The SS started shooting at the barge and people fell into the water, some of them living, some of them dead. Joe and I eased ourselves over the side and dropped into the water about ten feet below. The water in the Baltic Sea in early May is very cold, I can vouch for that!

Joe and I were in the water, clothes and all. Meantime the SS was raking the barge and the water with machine gun fire. The water was fairly shallow, just about chest high once we were half way to the shore. About one hundred feet or so from shore, Joe and I were wading, just about up to our waists in water, arm in arm, helping each other to move along to get to shore. Suddenly Joe slipped and fell over. I pulled him up and there from the side of his head was a stream of blood! He had been shot! I let him go and continued on to shore. There was nothing I could do for him. At least he did not suffer a slow death. But he is still in my thoughts.

The SS kept on shooting at the barge and at the people in the water. Then they lined up the survivors, including me, along the shore. Meanwhile, some of the SS found a row boat and rowed out to the barge, went aboard and fired their machine guns into the hold until there was no one alive. With the smell of gunfire and the moan of the dying in our ears we were herded along the road toward the town. I'll try to picture this for you. There was the bay with a long beach curving on for miles. Then on the shore, maybe 20 feet above the beach on an incline, was a paved footpath, about 20 feet wide, and above that was a road. That's where the SS walked, in front, along the sides and to the rear of us. We were on the footpath. Now you have to remember, we had had nothing to eat or drink for days. There were only two things keeping us moving ahead -- the fear of death and the hope for survival. And we kept on moving, one foot in front of the other, one foot in front of the other. Those who were at the end of their physical and mental strength fell by the wayside, to be shot by the SS, who were waiting for that opportunity.

What amazes me to this day is the fanaticism of these german SS guards. (At this stage I did not see any of the SS from the occupied territories.) The war was lost. germany was defeated. Hitler was dead! germany lay in ruins. But they carried on with undiminished brutality! However, this is not the time to go into my personal opinion of certain traits, which had come to the fore in a disturbing number of german individuals as well as their fellows. Also I don't want you to think that I don't know how to spell when I write "german" or germany with a lower case "g." In this context, I use the word german as an adjective and not as a noun!

The SS marched us for several miles until we finally wound up at an open field, probably their parade ground, with a number of barracks on each side. This turned out to be a german submarine school. By this time it was early in the afternoon. After a couple of hours, some thin soup was brought out in large pots and passed out among us prisoners. Before dark the SS surrounded us with machine guns and told us to lie down. I thought that this was it. This is the end of the road for me. But nothing happened!

MAY 3rd, 1945:
MY DAY OF LIBERATION!

The next day, the SS guards started to line us up again. Now there were maybe 300 of us left. They put us on a road, which led down to a pier in the harbor and started to march us down toward a small freighter. Several days before, another contingent of prisoners had been taken aboard another of these little coastal steamers, and blown up out in the bay. That ship's name was the "Ancona." All this we found out days later when we saw the half sunken hull of the ship. We also found out that the Captain of the little freighter that we were supposed to board, had refused to get under way because he claimed not to have enough fuel on board. Bless his heart and soul, for he surely saved our lives.

As we were shuffling down the road toward the pier, and we could surmise our fate, there was a lot of noise, cannon fire, air raid sirens, etc. "Everybody into the ditch!" "Off the road!" "Mach Schnell!" "Quick! Hurry! Hurry!" Were the germans afraid we might get killed? Ridiculous! I happened to lie in the ditch next to an SS guard. We assumed that this was another air raid. We had said it many times; we'd rather die from a Russian bomb than from a german bullet. But as the firing continued it became clear that this was not an air raid. Pretty soon shells were dropping here and there. The SS guard next to me said, "This is no air raid, this sounds like it's coming from inland!" No sooner did he say these words then the first British tanks came rolling down the street, their machine guns covering the road way! I disarmed the german guard who was lying next to me, as did other prisoners with their guards if they had the chance. It is amazing the amount of strength and courage one can summon if one's life depends on it! In reality, with the British tanks covering the guards, it didn't take much to grab the fellow's gun and hold him there. The initial British spearhead consisted only of about six or eight tanks of the Palestine Brigade, a volunteer Jewish outfit. The tanks kept the barracks covered with their guns while we disarmed the germans. Some germans who resisted were shot. And thus it came about that I was liberated on May 3rd, 1945.

The British soldiers, in the meantime had secured the german naval base with the help of reinforcements, which it seemed to us just came pouring in! We handed over the german SS guards, whom we had captured to the British. They were marched off along with the german naval personnel of the base, who had surrendered. And there was an end to the fighting and killing! The British army assigned us to a barrack on the base. A beautiful brick building with large bright rooms and toilets and showers and hot water and soap and beds with sheets on them, the likes of which we had not seen in years! It literally was as though we had died and gone to heaven!

We went out again in search of something to eat. Well, there wasn't anything around. The Jewish Armored Brigade to the rescue! The soldiers formed a chain out of each tank and handed out all the rations, cookies, chocolate bars, everything! I doubt very much that there was a single biscuit left in any one of the tanks! We tried to eat slowly, which was very hard to do, after not having even seen this kind of food in so long a time! We went to sleep that night as free men and with full stomachs.

The next morning I wanted to get up and walk around as a free man, but I was so weak and hot and I could not move. A British army doctor came and examined me and had me taken to the hospital with pneumonia. You'll remember that I had taken a swim in the Baltic Sea a few days earlier, so it really was no wonder that I should come down with pneumonia. Many others did also. And many died. I was very lucky that I made it. I was in the hospital about six weeks. Early on, I remember sleeping a lot or just dozing. Once in a while I'd open my eyes and there'd be a Tommy (an affectionate term for a British soldier) putting a piece of candy or chocolate on the cover of my bed! I still get a tear in my eye when I think of that gesture of kindness. May the Good Lord reward each and everyone of them!

During the time I was in the hospital, Red Cross people came around from bed to bed asking if there was anyone we wished to write to let them know that we were alive. When Hitler started to send Jews and other political objectors to concentration camps, my parents had decided that the Cardinal-Archbishop of Vienna, whom my family knew well, would be the most stable person in all this turmoil due to his position. We made a plan that should we get separated, we'd write to the Cardinal in Vienna and thus hopefully get reunited. And that is what I did. I wrote to Cardinal Innitzer or rather the Red Cross lady wrote for me. I told him that I knew that my father was dead, but that I did have some slight hope that my mother was still alive. That was early June of 1945.

In the meantime, my mother had been liberated in April 1945 by the Russian army in Auschwitz. She returned to Vienna in early June and of course had made contact with Cardinal Innitzer. So when word of my liberation reached her she was overjoyed and tried to get back in touch with me in Neustadt-in-Holstein. Shortly after the end of the war, the mail was highly erratic and some of my mother's letters were returned to her as undeliverable! One can only imagine her anguish at not being able to get the news of her being alive to me. I still have much of that correspondence.

NOVEMBER 1945 - FEBRUARY 1948: VIENNA

While all this was going on, a number of young boys, I among them, was selected to go to England as wards of the King. We were to be adopted by a British family and to receive a proper education and so forth. Altogether a wonderful opportunity and much to the credit of the King and the generosity of the British people, not in just words but in deeds! I myself shall be forever grateful to the British people for their much needed support at a very difficult junction of my life.

We were scheduled to go to London the end of October 1945. It was only a few weeks before I was to leave that I finally received word from my mother that she was alive and well in Vienna! So I immediately started to get my travel papers together to go to Vienna. I left Neustadt during the last week of October and arrived in Vienna on November 15, 1945, the day before my 18th birthday. I can still see myself walking into my Uncle Robert's apartment and the expression on my mother's face. The reunion was incredible! Neither of us ever expected to see the other alive. But yet, with the Good Lord's help, it happened. I had returned two weeks short of a four-year absence.

As I have said earlier, my mother was liberated by the Russian Army in the early part of April 1945 in Auschwitz (Poland), the notorious Nazi death camp. She arrived there in early 1945 after a torturous journey through camps in Poland and Germany. I had not seen her since we were in KZ Kaiserwald in mid 1944. She got back to Vienna sometime in early June 1945. That too was not as easy as you may think. The Russians like the British, French and Americans in their respective zones, were very suspicious and rightfully so of people who posed as refugees or Displaced Persons (DP's) as they were known, but in actuality were Nazi collaborators. As a matter of fact, these collaborators even infiltrated our post-war camps and applied to relief organizations set up to aid survivors of Nazi persecution. In our refugee camps we had our own interrogation committees set up to question and catch any imposters. Those we caught we turned over to the military government in charge of the particular area.

And so my mother got back to Vienna and after a while was able to secure a nice little apartment in the Inner City at Weihburg Gasse 21. It was near St. Stephen's Cathedral and the Archbishop's Palace where she worked. As before the war she worked for the Director of Caritas Socialis or Catholic Charities, as it is also known. After dinner at my Uncle Robert's and Aunt Steffie's apartment, that night of my return, she proudly took me to the home she had provided for her son.

It was a very, very nice one-bedroom apartment on the third floor, in the best part of town, one block away from the Stephans Platz. It had a sitting room, which now would probably be called a living room, a bedroom, a kitchen and also an alcove, off to one side in which I slept. In addition it had a balcony with a wrought iron railing, which ran around each of the upper floors, to which we had access through our living room door. The balconies were also accessible by staircases from the courtyard below. The courtyard was fairly large and had a number of trees and some grassy areas and probably flowerbeds in some earlier times.

I have to tell you a little more about this place. The building was about four hundred years old dating to the mid 1500's, a "converted" Franciscan Monastery. The walls were three feet thick. The modification probably was done in the early 1930s, but I am not sure of the date. It was very large, four stories with an inner court yard which one entered through an immense Portico in the front of the building. It was designed for a horse and carriage with enormous stone bumpers set into the two corners of the Portico to fend off the wagon wheels at the entrance to the building. It was to say the least an amazing place! This is where I spent a little over two years in Vienna, waiting to go to America! (Many years later, both of my children and their spouses took photos in front of Weihburg Gasse 21 on their trips to Vienna!)

After my return, the first thing my mother did was to hire a tutor to prepare me for my electrical engineering exam. She somehow did not think my "in the sand education" was enough, God bless her. After about a year or so of that, I sat for a four or five day exam and received my diploma. This was by special dispensation of formal classroom training for people in my situation, which was enacted by the Austrian Government at the time. It may be interesting to note that Emperor Franz Joseph I (circa 1890) had decreed that anyone studying for an engineering degree also shall have hands-on experience in the related trade. He insisted that his sons would go to college but would have a trade as well. And so I also hold Journeyman papers in my trade as an electrician!

By and large, the city of Vienna was spared large-scale destruction until the last few weeks of the war when Russian bombers hit a number of targets including St. Stephan's Cathedral. The roof of the church, with its beautiful ornamental tile work was totally destroyed. Also there was severe fire damage to the interior of the church. A number of buildings around the Square (Stephans Platz) were also completely bombed out. And on the Frantz Josephs Kai (landing), buildings lay in ruins. In addition there was considerable damage in many parts of the city. Almost every bridge across the Danube Canal was destroyed. However, the Reichs Bruecke (bridge), which my paternal grandfather had designed and built, was still standing across the big Danube!

My children and some of my friends ask me, "How did you feel about this destruction in your hometown?" Well, as a matter of fact, it did not bother me at all. I thought then and I still think that my compatriots at that time had it coming to them and then some! Remember the 98.7% vote by the Austrian people in favor of unification with Hitler's germany? As I traveled through germany on my way back to Vienna after my liberation, I came through a number of german cities, Hamburg in particular. I remember it well. You could see from one side of that town to the other, hardly one stone upon the other! To me, it was a beautiful sight! Do you think you could get much sympathy from the citizens of London for the inhabitants of bombed german cities after what Hitler did to London? I think not! Same here!

Now, I needed to get a job. I really don't know how this came about, but I applied to UNRRA for a job as a press photographer. UNRRA stands for United Nations Relief and Rehabilitation Agency. Being a press photographer was a skill I had acquired while being attached to the British army after I was liberated by them in northern germany. We were civilian employees of the British Military Government. We wore a military style uniform without insignias of rank, which gave us freedom of movement. A British photographer had taken me under his wing and had shown me how to use a Graphlex 4x5 Press Camera. I also learned from him how to develop film and use an enlarger to print photographs from negatives. So what had I learned there came in handy when I went to work for UNRRA in Vienna. I still have a few of the pictures, which I took at that time.

At any rate, here I was taking pictures in Vienna of the poor people, food lines, bombed buildings, etc. Pretty much the same as I had done with the British Army in germany. That was my job. But more than anything, this is where I met Wlodimierz (Jim) Russocki, who to this day is my best friend on this earth, with the sole exception perhaps, of my wife Marie, whom of course I did not know at that time!

I think from the moment we met, Jim and I were inseparable. I think we would have spent about eight or nine days a week together if that would be possible! When I think back about that time, I think it was just about the best time I had ever had thus far in my young life. I was about nineteen at the time. Jim was a year and a half younger than I. Consequently, Jim's mother trusted me to take care of little Wlodziu, that's Jim for short in Polish! And well she should have. He hardly ever tried to lead me astray, except that one time with the Colonel's daughter on Hubertus Hof! But let's not talk about that! We have been friends all this time -- now more than fifty years! And I'm glad!

From the very beginning after my return to Vienna my mother and I had applied at the US Embassy for emigration visas to the United States. Despite our background we had numerous interviews with the CID (the Counter Intelligence Division), the CIC (the Criminal Investigation Corps), and a number of others. At this point I'm no longer sure about all these initials. With all that, it took almost two years before my mother and I were granted our visas to go to the United States of America. The sole focus of my life then was to go to the USA, despite the fact that a number of people tried to encourage me to stay in Austria, including my former high school (Real Schule) principal, Dr. Hugo Bondy, who had become the Minister of Education in the new government. He assured me that with my political background I'd be sure to get a very good position within the ministry. I told him at the time, that I did not know two dozen people in the whole of Austria that I'd even shake hands with and for that reason, "I'm outta' here!"

For the sake of completeness of this record, from about mid June until December of 1947, I worked as an electrical engineer at a foundry in the 10th District of Vienna, which happened to be in the Russian Zone of Occupation. The foundry produced brass fittings and valves and such, a very interesting process. My mother was very worried about me working in the Russian Zone. I must admit she had good reason to be concerned. The Russians were known to pick up whole factories, from the production machinery down to the toilet bowls and sinks, including every man and woman in the place and export them to Russia as war reparation. Personally I had nothing whatever against the idea of the Russians getting whatever they could. It was just that my mother did not feel that I had to necessarily be part of that compensation! In all fairness, it is my understanding that the French, British as well as Americans received their share of war reparation in their zones of occupation, although, I trust, it was handled in a more "normal" manner. At any rate, the American Embassy had notified us that we were to obtain our visas within the next few weeks! Almost time to go to AMERICA! So I quit the foundry, ready to go to the US of A!!!

ANNA SOPHIA BOEHMERWALD: MY MOTHER

Before we leave Vienna altogether, I'd like to tell you a little more about my mother. She worked as she did before the war for Caritas Socialis at the Archbishop's Palace on St. Stephan's Square. My mother had the kind of compassion for the poor people who showed up in droves every day that this job required. A lot of people have compassion, but are not as willing to work at helping to make life a little easier for the poor. My mother would distribute donated clothing, some of it from America, or give a little food or money if such was available. On occasion we would get a truckload of potatoes, from where I do not know, but probably provided by our American friends. When that happened, some of the boys and I would be busy for a number of days, filling little sacks with potatoes to pass out to those who needed them. It was amazing how quickly word got around that a load of potatoes had come in!

And then there was this young priest who could not hang on to an overcoat! My mother would try to get him a coat and with luck would find one to fit him. But it was a sure bet that within an hour or less he would find someone whom he said needed it more than he did, and there he was without a coat again. My mother would find out about it and get him another one if possible.

If I recall correctly, my friend Jim left Vienna in the spring of 1947 to go to England via Italy to join the Royal Air Force. Before he left, he gave me his bicycle -- which by the way, was one of the first built in Austria after the war. Before my mother and I left for America I gave that bicycle to that young priest who could not keep a coat on his back. He told me that he would use it to take care of the sick and shut-ins of the Parish to which he was assigned. He also told me that he'd pray for me every day. I sure needed it and I was counting on it!

WINTER 1948 –
TO AMERICA!

As I said, I had a dream of what my life in America would be like. I want to tell you that it was better than I could ever imagine.

My mother and I came to the United States of America on February 21, 1948. It was a voyage that began on January 21, 1948, in Vienna, Austria. It was a very cold day. But it also was a very happy day. At long last, after more than two years of waiting to get our visa applications approved to enter the United States as legal immigrants, we were off to America!

We had a send-off at the train station by Bishop Jacob Weinbacher, an old friend, and many other priests and nuns with whom my mother had worked at Catholic Charities (Caritas Socialis). However, this send-off was by no means just for her. We were to be on an emigrant train of about 500 persons, many of whom were being admitted to the United States under the "Pope's Quota," namely for people who had been persecuted by the Nazis but who were not of the Jewish faith.

The train consisted of about 20 boxcars. And so 500 people, with all the belongings they had left and all the hope they could carry with them, were jammed into these boxcars. The train whistle blew, the engine chugged and around noon that day we were on our way to America; a trip, which would take a whole month!

Boxcar, cattle car, anything you want to call it, it is not meant by any means to be disparaging. Because, even though it was almost three years after the end of the war, passenger cars were practically non-existent, much of the rolling stock having been destroyed during the war. Each boxcar had an American soldier as guard and protector. Considering that the first 100 miles or so took us through the Russian zone of occupation in Austria, we all felt much reassured by his presence. Crossing from East to West was indeed an adventure! The border between the Russian and American zones lay across a railroad bridge. It was guarded by Russian troops who were under orders, as I found out shortly, to let no one across.

The bridge was an old wooden, single-track trestle. It seemed so narrow that the uprights of the bridge made it look like a tunnel. A one-way road to freedom! So near and yet so far. There had been rumors going around in Vienna that whole emigrant trains had been diverted at the border by the Russians and wound up in Siberia. Of course, I've nothing to substantiate these rumors. At any rate, the Russian guards signaled the train to stop and it came to a screeching halt. I can still hear that screeching of the brakes in the cold winter air and feel the dread of the potential peril that could lie in store for us!

The American officer, a Captain in charge of our military escort got off the train and walked forward to meet the Russian officer, also a Captain, in charge of the border crossing detachment. It was a tense moment. Neither could speak the other's language. We were at an impasse! The Russian soldiers drifted down the length of the train with their rifles at the ready. Our boxcars rode with their doors partially open for ventilation, and also so that people could look out at the scenery, if they should so desire, or leave the train for that matter, if it should stop. After all we were no longer prisoners, but immigrants on our way to America. Under these circumstances, it is easy to understand the Russian's concern to keep control of the situation.

I don't know why or how it happened, certainly nobody asked me to, but I got off the train, said a few words to the Russian soldiers guarding the train, and joined the officers and some other soldiers around a fire they had built to keep warm. In those days I was able to speak Russian quite well. After all, I had spent three and a half years in a german concentration camp with many Russian Jewish deportees and had worked along side, although not with, Russian prisoners of war and other assorted victims of Nazi terrorism.

So after having exchanged greetings, a few jokes and sung a few songs, some of which I translated for the American Captain, I asked the Russian Captain, since he had stopped the train, if he had food and water for the 500 people on the train. He told me that he hardly had enough food and water for his own soldiers, let alone for 500 more people. I explained to him, that if he wanted us to stay at this border crossing, he needed to come up with the necessary provisions. And I told him to let me know when he would be ready to feed the people on the train. There was a long pause and negotiations going on in the background between the Captain and some of his people. You have to understand that we were totally in the Russian's power. The American soldiers -- hardly more than two squads being lightly armed -- were not at all prepared for a standoff. Our American Guard Commander drifted away, kind of leaving things in my hands. I did not give it a thought nor could I blame him because in the circumstances he really could not be of much help. The situation must have appeared rather dicey, even from his perspective!

Meantime, I thought that this would be a good time to have a little more singing and story telling with the Russian soldiers. I don't remember the stories but I still remember the songs. Russians love to sing and they do it well. Some of the songs had a very fast beat and had funny little ditties. Others were slow and melancholy. There is nothing like a Russian tenor singing one of these. If you ever heard one sing "The Volga Boatmen," or "Stenka Razin," you know what I mean. It can really grab you.

All this had been going on for about an hour or so, during which time nobody had been allowed off the train. So after a while I asked the Captain again when he'd expect to have food and water for our people on the train. And again the Captain said that he did not know when the food would come, but that he was waiting for his Colonel to tell him. By this time it was about 5:00 p.m. and not much daylight was left. Something had to be done. NOW! I told him that I was not waiting for his Colonel and that I was moving the train out unless he could show me food for 500 people. The Captain told me that that was impossible and that he was sorry, but there was nothing he could do. This whole discussion, as all the ones before between the Russian Captain and myself, went on very amicably. No raised voices or anything like that. More like, "You can't get blood from a turnip!" "Charashoh!" OK! He understood that I had to do what I had to do. I'd like to send a special blessing and a sincere prayer for the good Russian Capitan. If it had not been for his forbearance this whole story could well have ended right then and there.

I got up from the campfire and signaled the train engineer to move the train out. I sat down again by the fire and we continued our conversation, talking about happier things, like how we conquered the germans! It took the train only a few minutes to start moving. It seemed like forever. By the time the train was well on the bridge, I got up, said good-bye to my Russian friends and first walked then ran after the train. They could have easily shot me. But they did not. Which again confirmed what my grandfather taught me when I was a little boy of seven or eight, about my grandson Michael's age. "Human beings are alright, but people stink!" I had just spent an hour or so with Human Beings! And so we crossed from the Russian into the American Zone of Austria and then on to Bremerhaven about 700 miles away in northern germany.

As my mother and I traveled westward toward a new life in America, on that cold January day, another journey inevitably came to mind. The journey my father, mother and I took some seven years earlier. Also in boxcars, but in a totally different direction and circumstances!

SEPTEMBER 1950 AND ON –
A PROUD AMERICAN

I am very proud to have served in the Army of the United States from September 1950 to September 1952, during the Korean War. Because I was an "alien," I had the option to decline. But it did not even enter my mind to refuse the call. After all, this is what I had come to this country for – to be free and to defend that freedom.

I rose to the rank of Staff Sergeant. My uniform is still in my closet and ready to go! I'd be happy to go to war for my country, in place of my son or my grandsons, if that were possible. But I suppose everyone has to fight his or her own battles.

After my discharge from the Army, I went to Manhattan College (now Manhattan University), a Catholic School. One Saturday night being sick and tired of studying I decided to go to the Newman Club dance at NYU. It was then and there that I met my future wife Marie. That was on December 12, 1952.

I became a citizen of the United States of America on October 30th 1953. That was a great day for me with my future wife, Marie, there to witness the occasion!

We were married on June 12, 1954. We have two wonderful children, Anne-Marie and John, Jr. Anne-Marie was born on May 29, 1955, and Johnny was born on May 22, 1958. We also have three terrific grandchildren. Anne-Marie and her husband, Tom Kendra, have two children, Michael Thomas and Alexis Marie. Johnny, as I still call him, and his spouse Karen have John Payne. Thank God, they are all well and healthy. The greatest blessing one could ever ask for.

Before we were married, I started on my 33 year career with IBM in the spring of 1954. My job with IBM eventually brought us to Austin, Texas in 1969. Marie and I are retired now for a number of years and enjoying our life.

1990 –A TRIP BACK TO VIENNA

In 1990, our son Johnny gave us airline tickets to visit Vienna. Bless his heart. Our trip to Vienna is the greatest gift anyone ever gave me! Still I must tell you, he had to talk me into it. A lot. But without that I would have never gone there. Consequently I would not have made my peace with the people of Austria. I think the importance in this is that you don't want to go to your grave consumed by hate of anyone.

I tried to show Marie a little of Vienna in the short time we were there. We were there 17 days but I could have used six months! One morning, Marie and I went to the Hof Burg, the Emperor's palace. One of the ornate buildings on the expansive grounds has been used for decades as the Chancellor's Residence. There, on the square in front of the Chancellory was drawn up a regiment of troops. There was a band, with trumpets, fifes and drums. The drums were pulled on little carts by donkeys. I looked at the soldiers drawn up there in rank and file. Now, you know how I feel about anything connected to the Nazis and their collaborators. And to some considerable extent that includes the Austrians. But these soldiers were KIDS, for heavens sake. Certainly not they and probably not even their fathers had anything to do with my past problems with the Nazis. I had to ask myself, "Am I going to carry hateful thoughts to my grave because of what their grandfathers may have done to my family?" No! These children are not in my debt! They are free of Nazi guilt and I wish them well.

THINGS I REMEMBER FROM BEFORE THE NAZIS TOOK OVER AUSTRIA.

THE OPERA BALL

As these things come to mind, I put them down as I remember them. When I was a boy about nine or ten years old, which makes it about 1936 or 1937, I received an invitation to the "Jugend Opern Ball" (Youth Opera Ball), which was held every year at the Vienna Opera House on the Ring Strasse. This was a formal affair of course, and just like all the other young lads of our acquaintance, I was decked out in my little tuxedo and ready for the ball. I still remember it well. There must have been two or three hundred kids lined up at the head of the stairs. The liveried Major Domo with his long staff in hand stood ready to announce each one of us in turn with three raps of his staff as we descended the staircase: "Herr Johannes Nicklas Peter Boehmerwald!" It was a grand affair!

My father, not long before the war, had taught me how to dance the Viennese Waltz. It was very simple. My dad made three chalk marks on the floor and from then on it was just, "one, two, three…one, two, three…" Well, anyway, I saw this nice girl and asked her to dance with me. I introduced myself and she said, "My name is Dorothea Hapsburg." I was dancing with an Arch Duchess of the Imperial House of Hapsburg! I was impressed but not overly so because I had known people like her all my life. However, since the end of World War I in 1918 and consequently the end of the Austrian Monarchy, aristocratic titles were no longer used except in the barber shop. A barber would never address one as anything less than "Herr Baron!" or "Herr Graf!" (Count) A poor tipper, I assume, probably would be just be a "Herr Doctor!"

AN OUTING TO THE VIENNA WOODS

I remember about the time when I was eight or nine years old, my parents and I went on an 'ausflug' (excursion) to the Vienna Woods, which is what we did most Sundays when the weather was good. We took along some blankets and a picnic lunch and bathing suits and had a great time. Sometimes we'd go with friends of my parents, but most often it was just the three of us. My dad helped me explore the woods and creeks, which ran through them, and he would teach me the names of all the trees and plants, which we came across. Also there were many castles and ancient ruins to explore! And my dad knew the history of them all along with many legends and stories, which he loved to tell!

On weekends when the weather was not so good my dad took me on long walks around the inner city to show me all the interesting places and tell me all the stories he loved so well.

The Glider Plane

On this particular Sunday in 1936, and I can still see it in my mind's eye as if it were yesterday, on our customary trip to the Vienna Woods, we came upon a large meadow. This meadow was very wide and long running down the side of a gentle hill toward some woods in the distance. Far away you could see the church steeples of Vienna and the silver ribbon of the Danube river. In the meadow there were a number of children with their parents. They were playing with something I had never seen before -- model airplanes – gliders! The children would toss their glider at a slight downward angle and the breeze coming up the hill would catch it and carry it aloft! These planes had about a four foot wing span, some bigger, some smaller, but they all were a marvel to me. I could tell my dad was also impressed, though he did not say very much.

During the following week there was all kinds of strange activity going on after I went to bed. I tried to find out of course, but nobody would tell me anything. Can you imagine my surprise, when next Saturday my dad came out of his den with a brand new glider! He had spent all week staying up late to build it for me. I don't think that in those days they had kits as we know them today. So he had to cut everything out from balsa wood by hand, just having drawings and plans and such. But being an engineer, he obviously was equal to the task. I was so proud that my dad did that for me.

The following day, which was Sunday, found us out there on that meadow. Our plane flew beautifully. It looped and soared; it was a wonderful sight to see. I was so happy.

THE RUIN MOEDLING

We now jump ahead to the summer of 1941. To the best of my recollection this was the last time my dad and I went on an outing together. My mother was not with us on this occasion. My dad took me to one of our favorite places, Moedling Castle. It was an old ruin of a 14th century Knights Castle. It didn't have a roof anymore and the moat had been filled in where the drawbridge used to be, but for a boy with a vivid imagination it was a great place. Naturally, my dad knew the history and all the legends of the place and I loved to listen to them. Moedling is a short train ride, only about ten miles south of Vienna, but I enjoyed riding the train, which had a steam locomotive and a loud whistle!

From the train station it was about an hour's hike up the mountain over wooded trails with wonderful views at occasional breaks in the forest. When we got to the castle my dad sat down on a big rock and started to write something on a piece of paper. After a while he finished writing and told me that he had composed a poem. He told me that it was not for me to read now but to come back when I had grown up and to read it then. He then searched the wall of rock and brick for some sort of crevice into which to deposit the poem. Finally, he found a suitable place, slid the paper inside, and wedged a sliver of rock into the crevice to protect and conceal it. He told me to mark the location in my mind very carefully. It was just about at my eye level and I also marked the distance from the corner of the wall on one side and the entrance door on the other. I had it all fixed very well in my mind!

After I returned to Vienna in November 1945, I went out to Moedling the following summer. Moedling was in the Russian Zone of Occupation, which in itself made this a somewhat dangerous undertaking, though well worth the risk. Try as I might I could not find the poem. It was not until years later that I realized that I had been looking in the wrong place. I was looking at my eye level, but I had forgotten that I had grown since that day in 1941. If I get another chance to go out there I'll try again. And if not, I'm sure my dad remembers what he wrote and he will tell me when I see him again!

FOR MY GRANDCHILDREN
I LEAVE THE ADVICE I RECEIVED:

FROM MY FATHER:

- Hard work and honesty will always be rewarded.
- Your good name is your most precious possession. Guard it well!

FROM MY MOTHER:

- Have faith in God, you will never be disappointed.
- Pray. Ask and you shall receive. Sometimes people who don't have, have not asked.

FROM MY GRANDFATHER:

- Be polite to everyone. A rude person no matter what his/her position has no class.
- Be punctual in all your dealings. Punctuality is the politeness of Kings.

FROM ME -- YOUR GRANDFATHER:

- Speak loud enough so people can hear you. But don't shout! A loud voice is neither a sign of authority nor of good upbringing.
- Plus all of the above!

They came first for the Communists,
and I didn't speak up because I wasn't a Communist.

Then they came for the Jews,
and I didn't speak up because I wasn't a Jew.

Then they came for the trade unionists,
and I didn't speak up because I wasn't a trade unionist.

Then they came for the Catholics,
and I didn't speak up because I was a Protestant.

Then they came for me,
and by that time no one was left to speak up.

by Pastor Martin Niemoller

Editor's Note

by Barb Tobias Chappell

More than 11 million people were exterminated during the Holocaust. Six million were Jews, three million were non-Jewish Poles, the remaining two million were Gypsies (Romany), Jehovah's Witnesses, Catholic Priests (3000 in Rome alone), communists, resistors and dissenters, and those deemed unfit to live (crippled, homosexual, mentally ill, etc.).

While it is true that for Hitler the catalyst of his mass maniacal eradications was his hatred of the Jews, there can be no denying that more than five million others were also exterminated during the Holocaust.

This story of Hans Nikolas Peter Boehmerwald (John P. Wald) is true. When Anne-Marie Kendra first showed me the words written by her father I was struck by their straightforward nature. Even as he captured his memories to paper, Mr. Wald's horrific story reads almost as a detached narrative. Only the original manuscript, punctuated by exclamation marks at the end of almost every sentence, belies his detachment. These marks stab at the paper as though to express the horror, despair and sadness he had difficulty putting voice to.

Mr. Wald was only 14 years old when he and his parents were taken away from their home and deported to concentration camps. Yet his bravery and cunning, which enabled him to survive, speak to a much older individual. "There were no longer any children in the camps," he says. Children were a liability. Those that were not killed soon died of the harsh camp conditions. Those that survived were forced to mature way beyond their years.

Anne-Marie and I took the utmost care in editing this story. These words are those of John P. Wald. We edited for punctuation and clarity of reading. We removed most of the exclamation marks, which had made the original manuscript very difficult to read. And we also corrected some of the verb tenses used. Since Mr. Wald's memoirs were written over a period of time, they contained several redundant paragraphs and anecdotes that jumped from time to time. We eliminated the redundancies and in some cases switched the order of the paragraphs for smoother chronological flow. Still, this is Mr. Wald's story as told in his own words.

As a Jew, I have been educated about the Holocaust since my earliest religious school memories. Still I had to be reminded that the Holocaust was not the Jewish people's story alone. It was my great honor to be asked to help with the editing of Mr. Wald's memoirs. And I thank Anne-Marie for sharing this important part of her life with me.

> The memory of evil will serve
> As a shield against evil;
> The memory of death will serve
> As a shield aginst death.

Elie Wiesel, Nobel Lecture, 1986

Hans Maximillian Boehmerwald,
Age 46   Vienna, 1938

Anna Sophia Boehmerwald,
Age 40   Vienna, 1938

Hans Nikolas Peter Boehmerwald
(John Peter Wald, Sr.)
Age 11 Vienna, 1938

Magistrat der Stadt Wien

Magistrats-Abteilung 61, Bevölkerungswesen

M.-Abt. 61 ~   **6 2 8 4 1**

~~Zum Amtsgebrauch für~~

S 1.— Verwaltungsabgabe entrichtet.

Wien, am   9. OKT 1947

Auszug
aus der Heimatrolle

Vom Magistrat der Stadt Wien wird bestätigt, daß

Hans Böhmerwald,

Beruf: *Mittelschüler*, Stand: *ledig,*

geboren am: *16.11.1927*, in *Wien,*

pol. Bezirk: *Wien*, Land: *Wien,*

am *) *13.3.1938*   das

Heimatrecht in Wien

(*JVa V-11699/26*) besessen hat.

Der Bürgermeister:
I. A.:

*) Zum Nachweis der Staatsbürgerschaft gemäß § 1 des Staatsbürgerschafts-Überleitungsgesetzes vom 10. VII. 1945, St. G. Bl. Nr. 59, ist u. a. der Besitz des Heimatrechtes am 13. III. 1938 erforderlich.
Die Einfügung eines nach dem 30. VI. 1939 liegenden Datums ist ungesetzlich, weil mit diesem Tage das Heimatrecht abgeschafft wurde.

John's Birth Certificate

74

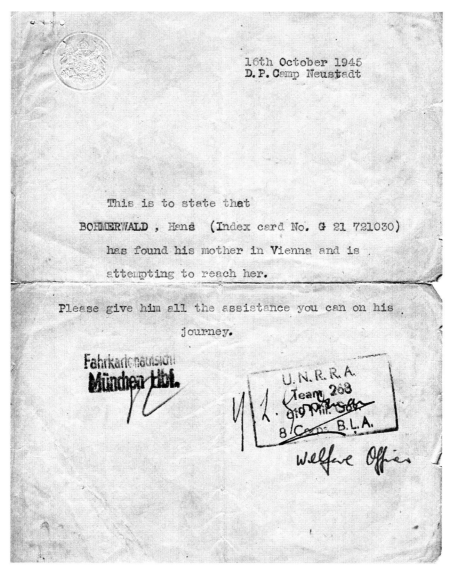

16th October 1945
D.P. Camp Neustadt

This is to state that

BOHMERWALD , Hans (Index card No. G 21 721030)

has found his mother in Vienna and is

attempting to reach her.

Please give him all the assistance you can on his

journey.

Fahrkartenausion
München Hbf.

U.N.R.R.A.
Team 268
g19 Mil.
8 Corps B.L.A.

Welfare Officer

After the war, the United Nations Relief and Rehabilitation
Administration (UNRRA) worked to facilitate the task of finding
loved ones for victims liberated from concentration camps
by providing them with notes like this.

The Bearer HANS BÖHMERWALD born 16.11.27. in Vienna AUSTRIA has been an inmate of the c.c. STUTTHOF and was liberated at NEUSTADT 3rd.May 45.

We ask that the Military and UNRRA authorities render every assistance possible to this party who is searching for his relatives.

268 UNRRA Team,
Neustadt/Holstein.
28.10.45.

Another UNRRA note.

12-1-46

№ 155970

UNITED STATES LINES COMPANY

AGENT

| 1. | 2. | 3. |
| 4. | 5. | 6. |

PASSENGER TICKET—(Not Transferrable)

ONE Class Ship MARINE TIGER

Scheduled to sail 2/0/08 19____

Embarkation from____ From Pier____

FROM BREMEN TO NEW YORK

NAMES OF PASSENGERS (This Passage is subject to terms printed, typed, stamped, or written below and on back of all pages)	Sex	Age	Room	Berth	Ocean Fare $	Taxes Collected
BOEHMERWALD HANS	M	20	C30	3	160	3

____Adults, ____Children, ____Quarters, ____Infants, ____Servants.

TOTAL OCEAN FARE $ 160

Issued at Bremen

By____

Date 4/2/48

TAX ___8

____TAX

Agent H.S.L. Bremen

TOTAL AMOUNT RECEIVED $ ___

By acceptance of this Contract Ticket, whether or not signed by him or on his behalf, or of passage on the ship, the passenger named herein agrees that the following terms and conditions, which are incorporated herein as part hereof, shall govern the relations between and be binding upon the carrier and the passenger in every possible contingency:

1. "Passenger" includes all persons named in this ticket as passengers. "Carrier" includes the ship, her owner, master, operator, demise charterer, and, if bound hereby, time charterer; "Baggage" includes all kinds of personal effects and property whatsoever of the passenger, whether or not remaining wholly or partly in the custody of the passenger, but does not include any articles such as are described in Clause 26. The rules and regulations and/or charges herein referred to are those promulgated by the Carrier or the agent whose name is subscribed hereto and for the time being in force.

2. Passenger shall be bound by and comply with the rules and regulations established from time to time by the Carrier or its agent respecting the transportation of passengers and their property, except to the extent, if any, of conflict herewith.

3. This ticket is not transferable. The passenger shall not be entitled to transportation except on production and surrender of this ticket or, in case of loss or theft of the ticket, only upon the furnishing of sufficient indemnity against use of the lost or stolen ticket. If this ticket is not used for the ship and sailing named herein, and the accommodations reserved are not released or canceled to the Carrier at least seven days before the scheduled sailing date, it shall be void and the passage money may be retained by the Carrier, except to the extent that the accommodations shall be sold to others.

4. The bed, berth or stateroom allocated to the passenger may be changed at the discretion of the Carrier or its representative at any time without notice. If accommodations are not available at the rate indicated on this ticket at the time that the passenger presents himself for transportation, the passenger will pay or receive, as the case may be, the difference between the rate already paid and the rate charged for the accommodations actually furnished. The Carrier also reserves the right at all times, if the accommodations occupied or to be occupied by the passenger shall be required for any person whose carriage is in the opinion of any officer or agent of the Government of the United States essential to the efficient prosecution of any war in which that Government may be engaged, to require the passenger to vacate such accommodations and to disembark forthwith at any port or place, and the Carrier shall not incur any liability of any nature whatsoever by reason of the exercise of the right reserved under this clause.

5. This ticket is good for the agreed ship only, but the Carrier in its discretion may substitute another ship, of the same or different ownership, at the port of embarkation or at any other port, and in such case, all terms and conditions hereof, in so far as may be, shall be applicable with respect to the substituted ship.

6. Prior to passenger's embarkation, Carrier, with or without notice to the passenger, may abandon the voyage or delay or advance the time of sailing, and in such case Carrier shall not be liable for any loss, damage or expense caused thereby, and in no event liable in excess of the price paid for this ticket.

7. After embarkation of passenger and prior to his arrival at final destination, Carrier may discontinue service between any ports, or omit any port, in the

(Contract Continued on Other Side)

John's ticket on the Marine Tiger, the boat he and his mother took from Bremen, Germany to New York City in 1948.

John and Anne's Austrian Passports

Inside of John's Austrian passport

Case No: . . . .

Subject: . . . . WALD . . . . JOHN P. . . . 125 W 70TH ST N.Y. 23, N.Y. . . . . . .
           (Name)   (First Name)   (Address)

To: International Tracing Service
      Headquarters
      APO 171   U.S.Army

From: American Federation of Jews from Central Europe, Inc.
      1674 Broadway
      New York 19, N.Y.

R E Q U E S T F O R C E R T I F I C A T E O F I N C A R C E R A T I O N
A N T R A G A U F I N H A F T I E R U N G S - B E S C H E I N I G U N G

(Please answer every question very clearly   (Jede Frage genau beantworten!
and write in Block Letters)   Bitte in Blockschrift schreiben)

Date MARCH 23RD 1955
Datum

INFORMATION ABOUT FORMER INMATE
ANGABEN UEBER DEN EHEMALIGEN INHAFTIERTEN

1. Name JOHN P. WALD
   Name

2. Maiden Name
   Maedchen Name

3. First Name JOHN P.
   Vorname

4. Sex MALE
   Geschlecht

5. Present Nationality U.S.A.
   Jetzige Staatsangehoerigkeit

6. Previous Nationality AUSTRIAN
   Fruehere Staatsangehoerigkeit

7. Birthdate NOV. 16TH 1927
   Geburtsdatum

8. Birthplace VIENNA, AUSTRIA
   Geburtsort

9. Last permanent residence before entering the Concentration Camp:
   Letzter staendiger Aufenthalt vor Inhaftierung in das Konzentrations-Lager:

   a) Place VIENNA II.   b) Street REMBRANDT STR Nr. 23
      Ort   Strasse   Nr.

   c) County VIENNA   d) Country AUSTRIA
      Kreis   Land

10. Marital Status MARRIED   11. Profession ENGINEER
    Familienstand

* * * * * * * * * * * * *

Turn
Wenden

In 1955, John filled out the requests for Certification of Incarceration (on this and the following 3 pages), one for himself and one for his father. This certificate enabled them to apply for compensation from the German government for the atrocities committed against them while incarcerated. They received a very small sum, in the neighborhood of $500-1000.

12. Information about the various stays in Concentration Camps:
Angaben ueber die verschiedenen Aufenthalte in Konzentrationslagern:

a) Above mentioned entered the Conc. Camp. *JUNGFERN HOF, RIGA*   Pris. Nr. *62473*
Obengenannter wurde eingeliefert in das Konz. Lager   Haeftl. Nr.
ARRESTED
on *DEC 1ST 1941*   coming from *VIENNA, AUSTRIA*
ARRIVED CAMP DEC 6TH 1941 von
am

b) transferred to Conc. Camp. *RIGA GHETTO*   on *AUG 1942*   Pris. Nr.
ueberstellt zum Konz. Lager *KAISERWALD, RIGA* am *JUL 1943*   Haeftl. Nr.
                                              AUG 1943

c) transferred to Conc. Camp. *SCHLOCK, RIGA*
ueberstellt zum Konz. Lager *KAISERWALD RIGA* on *FEB 1944*   Pris. Nr.
STUTTHOF D'ANZIG am *AUG 1944*   Haeftl. Nr. *62473*
STOLP, POMMERN   *SEB 1944*

d) transferred to Conc. Camp. *STUTTHOF, DANZIG* on *MAR 1945*   Pris. Nr. *62473*
ueberstellt zum Konz. Lager *TRANSPORT LÜBECK* am *26 APR 1945* Haeftl. Nr.

e) liberated, ~~released or died on~~ *MAY 3RD 45* in *NEUSTADT IN/HOLSTEIN*
befreit, entlassen oder gestorben am   in

13. Give the exact Name, Birthdate etc. used in the Conc. Camp if different from those on application
Geben Sie Ihren im K.Z. Lager verwendeten genauen Namen, Geburtsdatum und andere
Personalien, wenn von Ihren jetzigen Personalien verschieden.

NAME HANS BÖHMERWALD, CHANGED NAME TO WALD,
JOHN P. LEGALLT WHEN BECOMING US CITIZEN.

14. For which purpose is the certificate needed?   *RESTITUTION*
Fuer welchen Zweck wird die Urkunde benoetigt?

15. Any other useful Information
Weitere nuetzliche Angaben

16. Name, First Name and exact Address of person, to whom the certificate should be mailed
Name, Vorname und genaue Adresse, an wen die Urkunde gesandt werden soll.

WALD JOHN P. 125 W 70TH ST
N.Y. 23, N.Y.

17. What is relationship of enquirer to former inmate? *SELF*
Verwandschaftsgrad vom Antragsteller zum ehemaligen Haeftling?

Signature of the enquirer   *John P. Wald*
Unterschrift des Antragstellers
                            (Name and First Name in full)
                            (Name und Vorname ausgeschrieben)

Witnessed by:
Beglaubigt durch:

81

Case No: . . . .

Subject: . . . . BÖHMERWALD . MAX . . . .
         (Name)   (First Name)   (Address)

To: International Tracing Service
      Headquarters
      APO 171   U.S.Army

From: American Federation of Jews from Central Europe, Inc.
      1674 Broadway
      New York 19, N.Y.

R E Q U E S T   F O R   C E R T I F I C A T E   O F   I N C A R C E R A T I O N
A N T R A G   A U F   I N H A F T I E R U N G S - B E S C H E I N I G U N G

(Please answer every question very clearly   (Jede Frage genau beantworten!
and write in Block Letters)   Bitte in Blockschrift schreiben)

Date MARCH 23RD 1955
Datum

INFORMATION ABOUT FORMER INMATE
ANGABEN UEBER DEN EHEMALIGEN INHAFTIERTEN

1. Name BÖHMERWALD
   Name

2. Maiden Name
   Maedchen Name

3. First Name MAX
   Vorname

4. Sex MALE
   Geschlecht

5. Present Nationality AUSTRIAN
   Jetzige Staatsangehoerigkeit

6. Previous Nationality
   Fruehere Staatsangehoerigkeit

7. Birthdate MAR 31ST 1892
   Geburtsdatum

8. Birthplace BIELITZ, SELESIA
   Geburtsort

9. Last permanent residence before entering the Concentration Camp:
   Letzter staendiger Aufenthalt vor Inhaftierung in das Konzentrations-Lager:

   a) Place VIENNA II
      Ort

   b) Street REMBRANDT ST Nr. 23
      Strasse   Nr.

   c) County VIENNA
      Kreis

   d) Country AUSTRIA
      Land

10. Marital Status MARRIED
    Familienstand

11. Profession SALESMAN

* * * * * * * * * * * * * *

Turn
Wenden

82

12. Information about the various stays in Concentration Camps:
    Angaben ueber die verschiedenen Aufenthalte in Konzentrationslagern:

a) Above mentioned entered the Conc. Camp. _JUNGFERNHOF, RIGA_ Pris. Nr. ~~6247741~~
   Obengenannter wurde eingeliefert in das Konz. Lager   Haeftl. Nr.

ARRESTED
on _DEC 1ST 1941_ coming from _VIENNA, AUSTRIA_
am   von

ARRIVED CAMP DEC 6TH 1941

b) transferred to Conc. Camp. _RIGA, GHETTO_ on _AUG 1942_ Pris. Nr. _____
   ueberstellt zum Konz. Lager   am   Haeftl. Nr.

c) transferred to Conc. Camp. _KAISERWALD, RIGA_ on _JUL 1943_ Pris. Nr. _____
   ueberstellt zum Konz. Lager   am   Haeftl. Nr.

d) transferred to Conc. Camp. _SCHLOCK RIGA_ on _AUG 1944_ Pris. Nr. _____
   ueberstellt zum Konz. Lager _KAISERWALD, RIGA_ am _FEB 1944_ Haeftl. Nr.

e) ~~liberated, released or~~ died on _MAR 23RD 1944_ in _KAISERWALD, RIGA_
   befreit, entlassen oder gestorben am   in

13. Give the exact Name, Birthdate etc. used in the Conc. Camp if different from those on
    application
    Geben Sie Ihren im K.Z. Lager verwendeten genauen Namen, Geburtsdatum und andere
    Personalien, wenn von Ihren jetzigen Personalien verschieden.

14. For which purpose is the certificate needed? _RESTITUTION_
    Fuer welchen Zweck wird die Urkunde benoetigt?

15. Any other useful Information
    Weitere nuetzliche Angaben

16. Name, First Name and exact Address of person, to whom the certificate should be mailed
    Name, Vorname und genaue Adresse, an wen die Urkunde gesandt werden soll.
    ANNE S. WALD   125 W 70TH ST
    _N.Y. 23 N.Y._

17. What is relationship of enquirer to former inmate _HUSBAND_
    Verwandschaftsgrad vom Antragsteller zum ehemaligen Haeftling?

                    Signature of the enquirer _Anne S. Wald_
                    Unterschrift des Antragstellers
                                        (Name and First Name in full)
                                        (Name und Vorname ausgeschrieben)

Witnessed by:
Beglaubigt durch:

83

Vienna, January 18th, 1948

The Archbishiop of Vienna

Dear Mrs. Böhmerwald,

I am sincerely grieved to hear that you are
about to depart from our country with your son to
join your relatives over seas.

On this ocasion I express to you my sincerest
thanks as bishop, for all the work you performed in the
Caritas Welfare Center. Because you yourself were a
victim of the injustice of those dreadfull oppressive
days, our country suffered, you understood to give
true motherly care of to the poor and needy who turned
to you and you comforted and aided them. For all you
did and gave, I thank you most cordially. Mydear God
reward you and His blessings follow you into the
future. May he protect and guide you.

With blessings and good wishes,

s/ Th. Card. Innitzer

John's mother Anne, very active in Catholic Charities in Vienna
before and after the war, received this note from Cardinal Innitzer
before she left for the U. S.

Anne S. Wald
125 W 70 St.
N.Y. 23, N.Y.

Lebenslauf.

Ich, Anne S. Wald
vormals Anna Böhmerwald wurde
am 23. Jänner 1898 in Wien geboren.
Meines Vaters Name war Salomon
Wertheimer, meiner Mutter Name
Sophie Frankel. Ich besuchte in Wien:
die Volks- u. Bürgerschule u. die Sprach-
u. Fortbildungsschule Weiser.

Ich heiratete am 18. Febr 1923
meinen Gatten Max Böhmerwald, der
mich und unseren Sohn Hans Böhmerwald
erhielt bis zu unserer gemeinsamen
Deportierung durch die Nazi am
1. Dezember 1941 nach Jungfernhof
bei Riga.

Nachfolgend ist eine Liste

Letter from Anne S. Wald to Whom it May Concern documenting incarceration history. Translations follow.

von Lagern nicht Töten, wo ich meine Haftzeit vom 7. Dezember bis 10. März 1945 zubrachte.

7. Dez. 1941 verhaftet in Wien

6./XII 1941 – August 42 Jungfernhof b/Riga

August 42 – Juli 43 Riga, Ghetto

Juli 43 – Aug. 43 K.Z. Kaiserwald b/Riga

Aug. 43 – Februar 44 Arbeitslager Schlock b/Riga

Feb. 44 – August 44 K.Z. Kaiserwald Riga

Aug. 44 – Sept. 44 KZ Stutthof b/Danzig

Sept. 44 – Jän. 45 Sophienwalde Pommern

Jän. 45 Transport unterwegs nach Lauenburg wo ich am 10./III/1945 von der russischen Armee befreit wurde.

Mein Gatte Max Böhmerwald war mit mir u. unseren Sohn Hans zusammen in denselben K.Z. Lagern das ist vom 7. Dez. 1941 bis zu seinem Tode am 23. März 1944 im K.Z. Kaiserwald b/Riga. „Anna S. Wald

New York am 15. November 1954

(letter continued)

Anne S. Wald
125 West 70th Street
New York 23, New York
Life Story

I, Anne S. Wald, formerly Anna Boehmerwald, was born on January 23, 1898, in Vienna. My father's name was Salomon Wertheimer. My mother's name was Sophie Frankl. I went to elementary and secondary school in Vienna. I then went to the Weiser Language and Further Education School.

I married my husband, Max Boeherwald (sic), on February 18, 1923. He supported me and our son, Hans Boehmerwald until we were deported by the Nazis on December 1, 1941 to Jungfernhof near Riga.

What follows is a list of camps, with dates of my internment from December 1 (1941) until March 10, 1945:

December 1, 1941, apprehended in Vienna
December 6, 1941 to August 1942, Jungfernhof near Riga (Latvia)
August 1942 to July 1943, Riga Ghetto
July 1943 to August 1943, Concentration Camp Kaiserwald near Riga
August 1943 to February 1944, Workcamp Schlock near Riga
February 1944 to August 1944, Concentration Camp Kaiserwald near Riga
August 1944 to September 1944, Concentration Camp Stutthof near Gdansk (Poland)
September 1944 to January 1945, Sophienwalde, Pommern
January 1945, transported to Lauenburg, where, on March 10, 1945, I was liberated by the Russian Army.

My husband, Max Boehmerwald, was together with me and our son Hans in the same concentration camps from December 1, 1941, until his death on March 23, 1944, in Concentration Camp Kaiserwald, near Riga.

Signed Anne S. Wald

New York
November 15, 1954

Eidesstattige Erklärung.

Ich wurde in Wien am 1.12.1941 mit meinem Mann und Sohn
verhaftet und in folgende Konzentrationslager gebracht:
6.12.1941 in das K.Z.Lager Jungfernhof bei Riga, von dort
August 1942 nach Riga-Ghetto,
July 1943 nach Kaiserwald bei Riga
August1943 nach Schloch bei Riga
xAugust Febar 1944 nach Kaiserwald bei Riga,
August 1944 nachStutthof bei Danzig,
September 1944 nach Sophienwalde , Pommern
10.Maerz 1945 bei Lauenburg, Pommern befreit.Von dort bin ich
unter grossen Schwierigkeiten(teilweise durch Kriegshandlunge
zerstörte Eisenbahnverbindung etc.)nach Wien zurückgekehrt un
und im July 1945 angekommen.
Meine Gesundheit ist durch das Konzentrationslager dauernd geschädig
geschädigt worden:
1) Durch die mehrere Jahre dauernde Unterernährung in ausserster
Grad.Die Ernahrung wahrend dieser Zeit war nicht nur un-
zureichend, nicht ein Bruchteil der minimalsten Calorien-
menge, sondern haufig auch ungeniessbar.Unter anderen wurde
haufig gekochtes Ruhnerfutterete. ausgegeben.
2)Durch Unterbringung in ungeschuetzten Baracken, Kellern in
unfertigen Hausern etc.In den Winter-Monaten 1941/42 an
Jungfernhofwurden mehrere Personen taglich zu Tode gefroren.
3) Durch schwere koerperliche Arbeit wie Strassenbau, Kohlen-
schaufeln etc. die auch unter nomalen Umstanden und bei
ausreichender Ernahrung meine Krefte überstiegen hatte.
4)Ich wurde geprugelt und zu Boden geschlagen.Kaiserwald 1944.
5)Durch seelische Folter verursacht durch permanente Todes-
drohungen, Drohungen von Misshandlungen,
und durch den Umstand dass auch mein Kind und mein Mann, der
in K.Z. uns Leben kam, diesen Drohungen ausgesetzt waren.
Mein Mann starb am 23. Marz 1944 in Kaiserwald bei Riga.
6)Die ersten Symtome meiner Erkrankung waren heftige Schmerzen
und Schwellungen um den Gelenken und plotzliche Attacken von
starken Schmerzen in der Brust.
7)Ich habe bis zum Tode meines Gatten mit ihm in aufrechter
Ehe gelebt und habe mich nicht wieder verheiratet.

Documentation of incarceration by Anne S. Wald
(Translation follows)

88

Translation of documentation of incarceration by Anne S. Wald

Sworn Declaration

I was apprehended in Vienna on December 1, 1941 with my husband and son and was brought to the following concentration camps:

December 12, 1941 Concentration Camp Jungfernhof near Riga

August 1942 to Riga Ghetto

July 1943 to Kaiserwald near Riga

August 1943 to Scholck near Riga

February 1944 to Kaiserwald near Riga

August 1944 to Stutthof near Gdansk

September 1944 to Sophienwald near Pommern

March 10, 1945, liberated near Lauenberg near Pommern

From there on I had great difficulties getting back to Vienna because of ongoing war and broken-down rail connections etc. I arrived in Vienna in July 1945.

My health deteriorated because of my internment in the concentration camps.

1.) Over the several years of my internment, the nourishment given was not only not sufficient, but also not nutritious, and often, not edible at all. At times we were given cooked chicken-feed.

2.) Because we were living in unsecured barracks and unfinished housing, in the winter months of 1941 to1942 in Jungfernhof there were multiple deaths daily because of exposure.

3.) We performed hard physical labor, such as street construction and shoveling coal, etc., which under normal conditions and with normal nutrition would have been very difficult for me.

4.) I was physically assaulted and beaten to the ground in Kaiserwald in 1944

5.) My health also deteriorated through spiritual torture and continuous death threats and threats of torture, towards me and my son and my husband who died in the concentration camp on March 23, 1944 in Kaiserwald near Riga.

6.) The first symptoms of my deteriorating health were great pains and swellings in the joints and sudden attacks of great pain in the chest.

7.) Until the death of my husband I was in a bona fide marriage and I never married again.

MAXIMILIAN JOHN BÖHMERWALD
BORN 3/31/92 AT BIELITZ, AUSTRIA
SON OF ADOLF BÖHMERWALD &
HELENE BÖHMERWALD B. SILVERSTEIN
DIED K. 2 KAISERWALD RIGA LATVIA 3/23/44
ANNA S. WERTHEIMER (SOFIA)
BORN 1/23/98 AT VIENNA, AUSTRIA
DAUGHTER OF SALOMON WERTHEIMER &
SOFIE WERTHEIMER B. FRANKL

K2 12/1/41 — 5/3/45 JPW
12/1/41 — 3/10/45 ASW

Translation of incarceration history above, written by John Wald, Sr.

Maximilian John Boehmerwald (the husband)
Born March 31, 1892 at Bielitz, Austria
Son of Adolf Boehmerwald and Helene Boehmerwald, born Silverstein.
Died in Concentration Camp Kaiserwald, Riga, Latvia on March 3, 1944.
Anna S. Wertheimer (Sofia)
Born January 23, 1898 at Vienna Austria
Daughter of Salomon Wertheimer and Sofie Wertheimer, born Frankl
Concentration Camp December 1, 1941 to March 5, 1945 JPW
Concentration Camp December 1, 1941 to March 10, 1945 ASW

Max Böhmerwald

Geb. 31/VII. 1892 in Bielitz (Schlesien) röm. kath.

Zuständig nach Wien

Beruf: Weber

1898 bis 1906. besuchte ich die Normalklassen in Wien

1906 bis 1908 die Textilschule in Brünn

1908 bis 1912 Fa Max Kohn in Brünn
als Dessinateur

1912 bis 1913. Fa J. Pluss in Freiberg
als Musterweber

1913 bis 1919 eingerückt zum Militär
... ... mit ...

1920 bis 1936 selbständig in Wien

1937 bis Anfang 1938 Fa Werner Wien IV
als Schal u Kleiderstoff Weber
und Manipulateur

... ... bis zum
... ... gute Zeugnisse

(translation follows)

91

Translation:

Anna Boehmerwald, wife

Max Boehmerwald

Born March 31, 1892 in Bielitz in Schlesien (Austria at that time, but may now be the Czech Republic)

His legal residence was in Vienna and he was Roman Catholic

Occupation was a weaver

From 1898 to 1906 (aged 6 to 14) he went to school in NormalKleffern (illegible) in Vienna.

From 1906 to 1908 he was in Textile School in Bruenn (now in the Czech Republic)

From 1908 to 1912 he was at the Max Kohn Firm in Bruenn as a designer

From 1912 to 1913 he was at the J. Fluss Firm in Freiberg as a pattern weaver

From 1913 to 1919 he was in the German Army on the front lines, and was decorated for his service.

From 1920 to 1936 he ran his own business in Vienna.

From 1937 to the beginning of 1938, he was employed by the Werner Firm in Vienna in the Sixth District as a weaver and designer of scarves and dress cloth.

He was a master in his profession, able to work from the yarn stage through to the finished cloth, with great acclaim.

Anna Boehmerwald, wife
Born on January 23, 1898 in Vienna, where she also lived.
Occupation corsetmaker
She also made uniforms and artistic costumes, including leather flowers and leather belts and (following word illegible)
She owned her own sewing machine
Hans Peter Boehmerwald, son
Born on November 16, 1927 in Vienna, and attended one class of Real School, which is equivalent to our high school.

John P. Wald, Sr. with his wife Marie and their 3 grandchildren,
from left, Michael, Lexie and Payne.
The year was 2004, the occasion,
Marie and John's 50th wedding anniversary.

LaVergne, TN USA
21 September 2009
158612LV00002B/2/P